ST/ESA/315

m-gov

Department of Economic and Social Affairs

The Employment Imperative

Report on the World Social Situation 2007

United Nations
New York, 2007

DESA

The Department of Economic and Social Affairs of the United Nations Secretariat is a vital interface between global policies in the economic, social and environmental spheres and national action. The Department works in three main interlinked areas: (i) it compiles, generates and analyses a wide range of economic, social and environmental data and information on which States Members of the United Nations draw to review common problems and to take stock of policy options; (ii) it facilitates the negotiations of Member States in many intergovernmental bodies on joint courses of action to address ongoing or emerging global challenges; and (iii) it advises interested Governments on the ways and means of translating policy frameworks developed in United Nations conferences and summits into programmes at the country level and, through technical assistance, helps build national capacities.

PER
UNJ
ST/ESA
R25

Note

The designations employed and the presentation of the material in the present publication do not imply the expression of any opinion whatsoever on the part of the Secretariat of the United Nations concerning the legal status of any country or territory or of its authorities, or concerning the delimitations of its frontiers.

The term "country" as used in the text of this report also refers, as appropriate, to territories or areas.

The designations of country groups in the text and the tables are intended solely for statistical or analytical convenience and do not necessarily express a judgement about the stage reached by a particular country or area in the development process.

Mention of the names of firms and commercial products does not imply the endorsement of the United Nations.

Symbols of United Nations documents are composed of capital letters combined with figures.

ST/ESA/315
United Nations publication
Sales No. E.07.IV.9
ISBN 978-92-1-130262-2
Copyright © United Nations, 2007
All rights reserved
Printed by the United Nations, New York

Preface

Since the publication of the first issue of the *Report on the World Social Situation* in 1952, the series of reports have served as a foundation for discussions and policy analysis of socio-economic issues at the intergovernmental level. Over the years, these reports have identified emerging social trends of international concern and provided analysis of major development issues with national, regional and international dimensions.

The current issue, *Report on the World Social Situation 2007,* carries on that tradition by focusing on the subject of employment. More specifically, it surveys the global trends in employment and work, as well as the socio-economic context within which the world of work has evolved in the last two decades. The *2007 Report* examines the concept of full and productive employment and its relationship to socio-economic security and decent work, and highlights the critical importance of employment in achieving the overall goal of social development, and poverty eradication in particular.

The *2007 Report* closely examines four areas of increasing concern that are of particular importance when addressing the issue of employment: jobless growth, global informalization of the labour market, economic and social liberalization, and migration. It shows that these socio-economic trends are, for the most part, resulting in increased insecurity for workers. The *Report* analyses the impact of these trends on major social groups as well as the gender dimension of the changing labour market. It underscores the challenges faced by policymakers at the beginning of the twenty-first century with respect to achieving productive employment for all in developed and developing countries alike.

By providing an analysis of major challenges to achieving decent work and offering some policy directions for moving forward the employment agenda, the *2007 Report* strives to guide decisive actions at all levels aimed at building a more secure and prosperous society for all. Full, productive and decent employment is essential for achieving the internationally agreed development goals, including poverty eradication. Productive employment for all is not a policy option — it is an imperative for the twenty-first century.

SHA ZUKANG
Under-Secretary-General for Economic and Social Affairs

Contents

Figures

Tables

Boxes

Explanatory Notes

The following symbols have been used in tables throughout the *Report*:

Two dots (..) indicate that data are not available or are not separately reported.

A dash (—) indicates that the item is nil or negligible.

A hyphen (-) indicates that the item is not applicable.

A minus sign (-) indicates a deficit or decrease, except as indicated.

A full stop (.) is used to indicate decimals.

A slash (/) between years indicates a statistical year, for example, 1990/91.

Use of a hyphen (-) between years, for example, 1990-1991, signifies the full period involved, including the beginning and end years.

Annual rates of growth or change, unless otherwise stated, refer to annual compound rates.

Details and percentages in tables do not necessarily add to totals, because of rounding.

The following abbreviations have been used:

AIDS	acquired immunodeficiency syndrome
CIS	Commonwealth of Independent States
DAC	Development Assistance Committee
DHS	Demographic and Health Survey(s)
ECLAC	Economic Commission for Latin America and the Caribbean
ESAF	Enhanced Structural Adjustment Facility
EU	European Union
FAO	Food and Agriculture Organization of the United Nations
FDI	foreign direct investment
GATT	General Agreement on Tariffs and Trade
GDP	gross domestic product
GNI	gross national income
GNP	gross national product
G-7	Group of Seven major industrialized countries
HIV	human immunodeficiency virus
IFF	International Finance Facility
ILO	International Labour Organization

IMF	International Monetary Fund
NGO	non-governmental organization
ODA	official development assistance
OECD	Organization for Economic Cooperation and Development
PRGF	Poverty Reduction and Growth Facility
PRSP	Poverty Reduction Strategy Paper
SDR	special drawing rights
TB	tuberculosis
TRIPS	Agreement on Trade-Related Aspects of Intellectual Property Rights
UNCTAD	United Nations Conference on Trade and Development
UNICEF	United Nations Children's Fund
VAT	value added tax
WHO	World Health Organization
WIDER	World Institute for Development Economics Research
WIID	World Income Inequality Database
WTO	World Trade Organization

Reference to dollars ($) indicates United States dollars, unless otherwise stated.

When a print edition of a source exists, the print version is the authoritative one. United Nations documents reproduced online are deemed official only as they appear in the United Nations Official Document System. United Nations documentation obtained from other United Nations and non-United Nations sources is for informational purposes only. The Organization does not make any warranties or representations as to the accuracy or completeness of such materials.

Unless otherwise indicated, the following country groupings and subgroupings have been used in the *Report*:

Developed market economies:

North America (excluding Mexico), Southern and Western Europe (excluding Cyprus, Malta, and Serbia and Montenegro), Australia, Japan, and New Zealand.

Economies in transition:

Albania, Bulgaria, Czech Republic, Hungary, Poland, Romania, Slovakia, and the former Union of Soviet Socialist Republics, comprising the Baltic Republics and the member countries of the Commonwealth of Independent States.

Developing countries (49 countries):

All countries in Latin America and the Caribbean, Africa, Asia and the Pacific (excluding Australia, Japan and New Zealand), Cyprus, Malta, and Serbia and Montenegro.

Where data are from UNESCO, the following regional groupings have been used:

Arab States and North Africa: Algeria, Bahrain, Djibouti, Egypt, Iraq, Jordan, Kuwait, Lebanon, Libyan Arab Jamahiriya, Mauritania, Morocco, Oman, Occupied Palestinian Territory, Qatar, Saudi Arabia, Sudan, Syrian Arab Republic, Tunisia, United Arab Emirates, and Yemen.

Central Asia: Armenia, Azerbaijan, Georgia, Kazakhstan, Kyrgyzstan, Mongolia, Tajikistan, Turkmenistan, and Uzbekistan.

Central and Eastern Europe: Albania, Belarus, Bosnia and Herzegovina, Bulgaria, Czech Republic, Croatia, Estonia, Hungary, Latvia, Lithuania, Poland, Republic of Moldova, Romania, Russian Federation, Serbia and Montenegro, Slovakia, Slovenia, the former Yugoslav Republic of Macedonia, Turkey, Ukraine.

East Asia and the Pacific: Australia, Cambodia, China, Cook Islands, Democratic People's Republic of Korea, Fiji, Indonesia, Japan, Kiribati, Lao People's Democratic Republic, Malaysia, Marshall Islands, Myanmar, Nauru, Niue, New Zealand, Papua New Guinea, Philippines, Republic of Korea, Samoa, Solomon Islands, Thailand, Tonga, Tuvalu, Vanuatu, and Viet Nam.

Latin America and the Caribbean: Anguilla, Antigua and Barbuda, Aruba, Argentina, Bahamas, Barbados, Belize, Bermuda, Bolivia, British Virgin Islands, Brazil, Cayman Islands, Chile, Colombia, Costa Rica, Cuba, Dominica, Dominican Republic, Ecuador, El Salvador, Grenada, Guatemala, Guyana, Haiti, Honduras, Jamaica, Mexico, Montserrat, Netherlands Antilles, Nicaragua, Panama, Paraguay, Peru, Saint Kitts and Nevis, Saint Lucia, Saint Vincent and the Grenadines, Suriname, Trinidad and Tobago, Turks and Caicos Islands, Uruguay, and Venezuela.

North America and Western Europe: Andorra, Austria, Belgium, Canada, Cyprus, Denmark, Spain, Finland, France, Germany, Greece, Iceland, Ireland, Israel, Italy, Luxembourg, Malta, Monaco, Netherlands, Norway, Portugal, San Marino, Sweden, Switzerland, United Kingdom of Great Britain and Northern Ireland, and United States of America.

South and West Asia: Afghanistan, Bangladesh, Bhutan, India, Islamic Republic of Iran, Maldives, Nepal, Pakistan, and Sri Lanka.

Sub-Saharan Africa: Angola, Benin, Botswana, Burkina Faso, Burundi, Cameroon, Cape Verde, Central African Republic, Chad, Côte d'Ivoire, Comoros, Congo, Democratic Republic of the Congo, Equatorial Guinea, Eritrea, Ethiopia, Gabon, Gambia, Ghana, Guinea, Guinea-Bissau, Kenya, Lesotho, Liberia, Madagascar, Malawi, Mali, Mauritius, Mozambique, Namibia, Niger, Nigeria, Senegal, Sierra Leone, Togo, Uganda, Rwanda, Sao Tome and Principe, Seychelles, Somalia, South Africa, Swaziland, United Republic of Tanzania, Zambia, and Zimbabwe.

Least developed countries:

Afghanistan, Angola, Bangladesh, Benin, Bhutan, Burkina Faso, Burundi, Cambodia, Cape Verde, Central African Republic, Chad, Comoros, Democratic Republic of the Congo (formerly Zaire), Djibouti, Equatorial Guinea, Eritrea, Ethiopia, Gambia, Guinea, Guinea-Bissau, Haiti, Kiribati, Lao People's Democratic Republic, Lesotho, Liberia, Madagascar, Malawi, Maldives, Mali, Mauritania, Mozambique, Myanmar, Nepal, Niger, Rwanda, Samoa, Sao Tome and Principe, Senegal, Sierra Leone, Solomon Islands, Somalia, Sudan, Timor-Leste, Togo, Tuvalu, Uganda, United Republic of Tanzania, Vanuatu, Yemen, and Zambia.

Introduction

> We commit ourselves to promoting the goal of full employ-
> ment as a basic priority of our economic and social policies,
> and to enabling all men and women to attain secure and
> sustainable livelihoods through freely chosen productive
> employment and work.
>
> *— Commitment 3 of the Copenhagen Declaration on*
> *Social Development, adopted by the World Summit*
> *for Social Development, Copenhagen, 1995*

Since the World Summit on Social Development — held in Copenhagen from
6 to 12 March 1995, the United Nations has underscored the role of productive
employment in reducing poverty and promoting social development. At the
2005 World Summit held in September 2005, world leaders had undertaken
the commitment "to make the goals of full and productive employment and
decent work for all, including for women and young people, a central objective
of (their) relevant national and international policies".[1] Moreover, in paragraph
5 of the ministerial declaration adopted by the Economic and Social Council
on 5 July 2006, Members and Heads of Delegations participating in the high-
level segment resolved to promote full and productive employment and decent
work for all.[2] Further, the Secretary-General has, in his report on the work of
the Organization issued in 2006, proposed to include a new target, echoing the
above-mentioned commitment of the 2005 World Summit, under Millennium
Development Goal 1.[3]

At the core of the United Nations approach to full and productive employment and decent work, is the Universal Declaration of Human Rights[4] which
states in article 23(1) that everyone has the right to work, to free choice of
employment, to just and favourable conditions of work and to protection against
unemployment. Ensuring free choice of employment means enabling people to
work out their own work trajectories over their working lives. Choice is about
the absence of coercion and control, or other social obstacles to the exercise of
one's capacities. Since choice matters, policymakers should seek to create policies

and institutions that improve choice for all people. To spread decent work, policymakers should start by developing strategies designed to strengthen economic freedom and rights instead of merely focusing on overall job creation.

However, it should be stressed that unemployment is a weak indicator of decent-work deficits. In most of the developing world, "employment" and "unemployment" are crude measures, at best, of the state of people's livelihoods and well-being. The reality is that in developing countries, most people simply cannot afford to be unemployed. The focus in developing economies should therefore be not only on unemployment and unemployment indicators but also on underemployment and under paid employment.

Also, the notion of employment is increasingly being replaced by the concept of sustainable livelihoods. The notion of employment traditionally refers to a stable wage relationship, whereas sustainable livelihoods encourages us to think more about how people work and how they wish to work. The notion of sustainable livelihoods conveys the idea that development and work should be seen as integrated sets of activities that entail more than just the earning of incomes (Scoones and Wolmer, 2003). The term refers to the range of linked activities potentially undertaken by most people, including domestic work (such as caregiving), paid labour, commuting to and from working activity, petty trading, labour circulation, social networking, secondary work, voluntary community work, charitable work, and the various activities associated with learning skills, training and the dissemination and receiving of information.

The notion of decent work has become part of the lexicon of work and labour analysis since it was introduced by the International Labour Organization (ILO) in 1999. Decent work for the person performing it should be satisfying, that is to say, it should promote personal development and contribute to the well-being of society as well as to the well-being of his or her family. A society committed to the promotion of decent work would be one in which people are living in conditions of basic economic security and of equality of good opportunity to develop and apply their competencies safely and with a broadening range of economic, social and cultural rights.

More specifically, decent work involves opportunities for kinds of work that are productive and that deliver fair incomes, security in the workplace and social protection for families, better prospects for personal development and social integration, freedom for people to express their concerns, organize and participate in decisions that affect their lives, and equality of opportunity and of treatment for all women and men.

In each of these areas, people throughout the world face deficits, gaps and exclusions in the form of unemployment and underemployment, poor-quality

Dimensions of socio-economic security and decent work [a]	
Decent work	**Socio-economic security**
1. **Opportunities for work** (the need for all persons [men and women] who want work to be able to find work)	**Labour-market security** (adequate employment opportunities)
2. **Productive work** (essential for workers to have acceptable livelihoods for themselves and their families, and essential to ensure sustainable development and competitiveness of enterprises and countries)	**Basic needs security** (capacity for safeguarding one's subsistence or basic well-being) **Job security** (a niche designated as an occupation or "career") **Skill reproduction security** (opportunities to gain and retain skills) **Income security** (protection of income through minimum wage machinery, wage indexation, comprehensive social security, taxation to reduce inequality)
3. **Security at work** (the need to help safeguard health, pensions and livelihoods, and to provide adequate financial and other protection in the event of health and other contingencies. This also recognizes workers' need to limit insecurity associated with the possible loss of work and livelihood)	**Employment security** (protection against arbitrary dismissal, etc.) **Work security** (protection against accidents and illness at work, through safety and health regulations, and limits in working time, unsocial hours, night work for women, etc.)
4. **Dignity at work** (workers should be treated with respect at work, and should be able to voice concerns and participate in decision-making about working conditions)	**Security of representation** (protection of the collective voice, independent trade unions and employers' associations)
5. **Work in conditions of freedom** (work should be freely chosen and not forced on individuals, it being understood that certain forms of work are not acceptable in the twenty first century. This means that bonded labour and slave labour as well as unacceptable forms of child labour should be eliminated as agreed by Governments in international declarations and labour standards. It also means that workers are free to join workers' organizations)	**Work in conditions of freedom** (work should be freely chosen and not forced on individuals, it being understood that certain forms of work are not acceptable in the twenty first century. This means that bonded labour and slave labour as well as unacceptable forms of child labour should be eliminated as agreed by Governments in international declarations and labour standards. It also means that workers are free to join workers' organizations)
6. **Equity in work** (workers need to have fair and equitable treatment and opportunity at work. This encompasses the absence of discrimination at work and access to work and the ability to balance work with family life)	By definition, this dimension of decent work is implicitly included in the socio-economic security paradigm

[a] Adapted from: Igor Chernyshev, *Socio-Economic Security and Decent Work in Ukraine: A Comparative View and Statistical Findings*, "Working Paper, No. 76, (Geneva, Policy Integration Department, Statistical Development and Analysis Group, International Labour Office, October 2005).

and unproductive jobs, unsafe work and insecure income, rights that are denied, gender inequality, exploitation of migrant workers, lack of representation and voice, and inadequate protection and solidarity in the face of disease, disability and old age.

Economic security creates good opportunities for decent work, as reflected in activities that are freely chosen. Without such security, people cannot develop their capabilities because, often, they have to take what is readily available, rather than hold out for work that might better suit their skills, background, education and preferences. Without security, they have to curtail their creative and productive work preferences excessively.

Socio-economic security means assured access to basic needs, such as food, water, housing and schooling, coupled with access to good opportunities to pursue productive and creative work in a decent way. A crucial concern is that such activity should be freely chosen to the extent that is feasible, and the trend should be towards greater freedom, rather than less.

The table on the previous page displays the intersecting dimensions of socio-economic security and decent work, and demonstrates that it is the combination of forms of security that could make decent work a reality.

In the first decade of the twenty first century, the world is faced with a series of challenges with respect to work and labour. At root, the broad economic and social context determines how one thinks about work. Every human being has the right to be able to work under decent conditions; but there are always trade-offs, and it would be utopian to imagine that work and labour could be as enjoyable as most of us might wish it to be.

Policies should be devised to ensure that conditions of work steadily improve, especially for those obliged to do the lowest-paid and most onerous forms of labour and work. This is why socio-economic security should be given high priority, for only in a context of such security can people make decent choices and have the option of refusing to put up with degrading or debilitating labour.

Findings

The basic tenet of the World Summit for Social Development encompassed the creation of a "society for all". The notion of "decent work for all" is a logical

corollary of that principle. Today, the world of work is being profoundly transformed. Sectoral shifts, in themselves, are making the old images of full-time,
single-occupation labour and employment inappropriate as guides to the future.
Labour markets evolve all the time, but the evidence is that in the current phase
of globalization, they have been evolving in the direction of greater levels of economic insecurity and greater levels of most forms of inequality, many of which
have a direct adverse effect on the opportunity of people to live a life of decent
work and satisfactory employment.

Social cohesion and political stability are important for economic stability,
investment and growth and, ultimately, for the health of the labour market and
employment opportunities and conditions. Income inequality can compromise
social cohesion, lead to political violence and endanger government stability. In
other words, income inequality contributes to a political and social environment
that is not conducive to decent work and full employment. The fact that, uti-
mately, lowered social cohesion strains institutions and impedes growth negatively impacts labour-market conditions and is likely to further fuel income
inequality.

The statistics are not encouraging: it is estimated that in 2006, 1.4 billion
of those working did not earn enough to lift themselves and their families above
the two dollars–a-day poverty line. This figure includes about 507 million workers and their families who lived below the one dollar–a-day poverty line.

Many of the world's youth live in poverty. It is estimated that one-fifth of
the total global youth population (over 200 million persons) live on less than
$1 per day, and that roughly one in every two young men and women (515 mil-
lion persons) live on less than $2 per day. The plight of the working poor among
young people is an issue that has only recently started to gain attention. Furthermore, roughly 1 in every 10 young persons, or a total of 130 million young people, are illiterate, having missed out on, or having been forced to drop out of,
primary education during their childhood.

Of the 650 million persons with disabilities, about 470 million are of working age. They are much more likely to be unemployed or underemployed than
persons without disabilities. Workers with disabilities tend to fare less well than
other workers, especially when unemployment rises. Persons with disabilities are
much more likely than those without disabilities to live in poverty, and of the
1.4 billion people surviving on less than $2 a day, persons with disabilities are

often among the poorest. There is a strong correlation between poverty and disability, as people who are living in poverty are more likely to become disabled, and persons with disabilities are more likely to be poor.

Indigenous peoples are disproportionately represented among the poorest of society. Although indigenous peoples make up only 5 per cent of the world's population, they represent about 15 per cent of the world's poorest; and although labour statistics are frequently not disaggregated by ethnicity, in most countries unemployment rates among indigenous peoples seem to be significantly higher than the national average.

Promoting and generating full employment and decent work for all are increasingly seen as constituting crucial pathway towards achieving the Millennium Development Goals, especially the goal of poverty reduction. However, as this report will show, there are many challenges to be met and obstacles to be overcome in reaching the poorest, the most marginalized and, by implication, the most excluded.

The advance of globalization has had important implications for work and employment outcomes in all countries. However, changes in international and national markets for labour have presented different sets of challenges for different groups in society. Some of the social groups that are more visible than others have managed to dominate the debate on work and labour. The lack of visibility of other groups requires vigorous and sustained action to ensure that their particular concerns and challenges are recognized and adequately addressed by policy-makers. Therefore, giving voice to all members of society, including workers and the unemployed, women, migrants and other marginalized groups, should ensure that their views on matters affecting their lives are heard.

However, this will not be an easy matter. Governments and employers around the world, in their determination to remain or become economically competitive, have taken numerous steps to increase external labour-market flexibility, and in doing so, have engendered greater insecurity among most groups of workers. An extremely flexible system is likely to be a highly unstable one and, above all, the global trend towards employment flexibility means that fewer workers can anticipate being in stable, protected employment.

Furthermore, there has been an informalization of employment and work in many parts of the world. In contrast with past experience, economic growth has not been strongly associated with the growth of formal employment; indeed, informal activities, however defined, seem to have grown in absolute and relative terms. In fact, the world as a whole as well as many countries seem to be suffering from "jobless growth". In other words, the economy is growing without any jobs being generated or with a diminishing number of jobs created for any particular rate of economic growth.

Informalization is closely linked to labour casualization. Labour-market restructuring, often creating greater flexibility in the labour market, has increasingly led to the spread of precarious labour relationships, especially employment insecurity, which manifests itself in various forms. Globally, there has been a spread of short-term contracts, giving workers fewer entitlements and little sense of security in their employment. Extensive casualization has long characterized labour relationships in developing countries, but in recent decades it has been growing everywhere. Often, workers retain temporary status even though they have remained in their jobs for many years. The fact that these workers face constant insecurity makes them less inclined to object to workplace changes to wage cuts or to loss of benefits, out of fear of losing their jobs.

The recent deregulation, privatization and marketization of social services have had profound effects on labour markets and employment sectors that had set standards of social security for several generations. This transformation of social services has been a crucial dimension of the transformation of labour and work across the world.

Workers providing social services have tended to experience reductions in employment security and income security, and have tended to lose voice and representation, inasmuch as private sector workers are much less likely to be unionized or to enjoy such workplace safeguards as have been the norm in the public sector. Liberalization and privatization have meant that "permanent" employment, characteristic of civil services until a few years ago, has been diminishing rapidly. Many more workers have been placed on short-term contracts, with periods of short notice for dismissal. Outsourcing and subcontracting have become far more common. All these changes may have helped to reduce labour costs, but at the same time they have created many more insecurities for those providing the services.

Standardized contracts and collective contracts are giving way to more individualized contracts based on bargaining on an individual level between employers and workers. One concern is that since the bargaining strengths of managers and individual workers differ enormously, a shift to more decentralized and individualized employment relations must tilt the balance in favour of employers.

This shift of power to employers is further underpinned by the globalization of financial markets, which makes it more difficult to tax relatively mobile factors of production such as capital. In effect, taxation on capital has been falling, while the effective tax share borne by labour income has been rising, further worsening the functional income distribution. Furthermore, and also as a result of globalization, there has been a greatly increased abundance of labour supply. This abundant globalized labour supply contributes to keeping down wages: employers can always impose pay cuts merely by threatening to shift production to lower-income countries.

International labour mobility has lagged significantly behind international capital mobility. Nonetheless, there are signs that a new global labour market is emerging. For managerial and professional workers, the enhanced opportunity for international mobility is unquestionably advantageous. Many of those who are moving around have obtained secure employment contracts with national or multinational corporations. Others move from contract to contract, with high incomes and access to private benefits and investments. However, for many others who have fewer skills, there are various forms of insecurity and deprivation associated with their labour mobility.

Another important factor is the trend away from statutory regulation to self-regulation as part of the liberalization that has accompanied globalization. Self-regulation may engender greater work insecurity. With liberalization, there has been a steady rollback in State systems of social security and reduced expectations of the universality of State provision. Although these reversals have been observed almost everywhere, they have been strongest in some of the most developed "welfare state" countries, and have been evident as well in middle-income and developing countries, which had previously been expected to develop State-based social security systems.

The concept of social insurance has always been the cornerstone of social security systems. However, social insurance is automatically weak in economies dominated by informal economic activities and is surely being weakened further by the growth of more flexible labour relations. In such circumstances, it is unrealistic to envisage social insurance as the cornerstone of social protection in the future, given the growing informalization, labour casualization, offshoring and labour-market flexibility that are all part of the pursuit of the economic liberalization that defines globalization.

Recommendations

Policies and strategies devised to promote and generate full employment and decent work should take into account the issue of inequality, as there are linkages between inequalities and the achievement of full employment and decent work. Addressing economic, social and political inequalities that underlie labour-market performance as well as the corresponding impact of the labour market on inequalities should underpin policy considerations. Taking these synergies and compensating mechanisms into account is therefore essential in developing policy packages and in shaping political support.

The design of policies able to promote employment and decent work also needs to reflect the demographic and social changes in society, such as the growth in the number of youth and older people, the growth of households headed by single-women, and the displacement of indigenous peoples from environments in which they had survived for so long. For example, policies that do not take into account the number of older people as well as the increasing proportion of youth in the population could create biases against such workers, thereby generating increasing unemployment in their age cohorts, while disregarding the higher productivity that older workers may offer to society. Similarly, policies that fail to account for the growing number of households headed by single women by, *inter alia*, not providing chilecare and family health benefits, could fail to increase the number of women in employment.

Political reforms and legal provisions for recognizing greater equality in respect of race, gender and age are also essential for raising businesses' awareness and consciousness of these objectives. The protection of immigrants' workplace rights and civil rights should be embedded in immigration laws and reflected in the enforcement of equal employment opportunity provisions. In fact, the introduction of anti-discrimination laws is needed to ensure that employment growth and decent work do not disproportionately benefit the more privileged members of society.

Social protection systems also need to adapt to more flexible labour-market conditions in order to provide economic security to all workers. With more and more workers in employment situations that are casual, informal and outside of standard collective contracts, either by choice or by necessity, universality of coverage becomes even more important. In addition, the broadening of the concept of work to include unpaid work demands new ways of thinking about eligibility for participation in, and contribution to, social protection systems.

Finally, it is worth reiterating that it is decent work for all, rather than economic growth *per se*, or even simple job creation that should be placed at the centre of economic and social policy-making. Such a paradigm shift is the starting point for the fundamental change that is needed. International institutions, especially those in the United Nations system, should actively promote the shift and incorporate its underlying principle in their own activities.

Notes

[1] See General Assembly resolution 60/1 of 16 September 2005, para. 47.

[2] See *Official Records of the General Assembly; Sixty-First Session, Supplement No. 3* (A/61/Rev.1), chap. III, para. 50.

[3] Ibid., *Supplement No. 1* and corrigendum (A/61/1 and corr.1), para. 24.

[4] General Assembly resolution 217 A (iii) of 10 December 1948.

Chapter I

Global employment and work

Over the last decade, global employment has been rising slowly, accompanied by increasing global unemployment and continuing pervasive poverty. These trends underscore the inability of the current global economy to generate adequate levels of productive employment and decent work. At the same time, labour markets almost everywhere are being made more flexible as social protection has generally declined, with some notable exceptions.

Globally, the understanding of labour-market developments has been made more difficult by complex and varied labour-market and work trends, with an apparent spread of labour-market informalization in many countries, new types of work and work arrangements emerging in service economies, and, according to anecdotal evidence, more activity taking place in the shadow economy, outside the reach of taxes, regulation and measurement. Essentially, within the global transformation, there have been a series of redivisions of labour, which will be considered in the following sections.

Global employment and unemployment trends

Between 1996 and 2006, the global labour force, consisting of people who were either working or looking for work, had grown by 16.6 per cent, to 2.9 billion, based on International Labour Organization (ILO) estimates.[1] That labour force represented about two thirds of the 4.6 billion people of working age (aged 15 years or over) in 2006.

Over the same period, the unemployment rate worldwide rose from about 6.0 to 6.3 per cent. The number of unemployed worldwide rose to 195 million people in 2006, from 161.4 million in 1996 (see figure I.1). This increase occurred even though global economic output had grown at the rate of 3.8 per cent per annum, giving rise to the phenomenon "jobless growth", discussed below.

Furthermore, it is estimated that in 2006, 1.4 billion of those working did not earn enough to lift themselves and their families above the two dollars-a-day

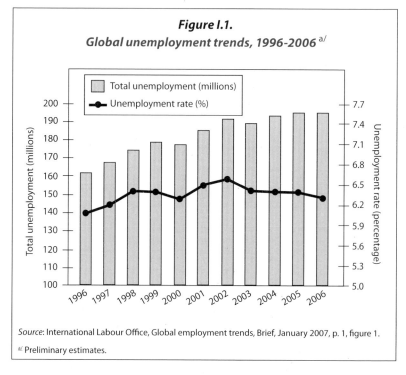

Figure I.1.
Global unemployment trends, 1996-2006 [a]

Source: International Labour Office, Global employment trends, Brief, January 2007, p. 1, figure 1.

[a] Preliminary estimates.

poverty line. This figure includes about 507 million workers and their families who lived below the one dollar-a-day poverty line. Worldwide, the percentage of the two dollars-a-day working poor in total employment decreased to 47.4 in 2006, from almost 55 in 1996, although significant regional differences have persisted (see table I.1).

Global demographic forces have had a significant impact on the employment and unemployment situations. The contrast between the ageing populations and declining birth rates in developed countries, and the younger populations and relatively higher fertility rates in developing countries, has been reflected in different demographic and labour supply consequences.

Over the last decade, there has been a slight decline in the share in employment of the world's working-age population (aged 15 years or over), to 61.4 per cent in 2006 from 62.6 per cent in 1996. However, the decrease was larger among young people (aged 15 - 24). Within this group, the ratio decreased from 51.0 per cent in 1996 to 46.8 per cent in 2006. The increasing proportion of young people in education may explain this reduction in part. The gap between men and women continued: in 2006, 48.9 per cent of women were employed,

Table I.1.
Indicators of the working poor

Year	1996	2001	2006*	1996	2001	2006*
	(millions)	(millions)	(millions)	Share in total employ-ment (%)	Share in total employ-ment (%)	Share in total employ-ment (%)
US$ 1 a day working poor						
World	594.6	5786	5070	24.0	21.7	17.6
Central and Eastern Europe (non-EU) and CIS	12.4	10.3	3.5	7.5	6.2	2.1
East Asia	145.0	147.0	950	20.3	19.6	12.1
South-East Asia and the Pacific	37.4	30.9	29.6	17.0	12.7	11.1
South Asia	250.8	222.3	196.9	53.8	43.2	34.4
Latin America and the Caribbean	22.9	27.4	27.2	12.1	12.7	11.3
Middle East and North Africa	2.6	3.4	3.5	3.0	3.3	2.8
Sub-Saharan Africa	123.5	137.3	151.3	57.3	56.9	55.4
US$ 2 a day working poor						
World	1354.7	1394.1	1367.8	54.8	52.2	47.4
Central and Eastern Europe (non-EU) and CIS	54.5	51.4	18.0	33.0	31.0	10.5
East Asia	442.9	412.6	347.2	61.9	55.0	44.2
South-East Asia and the Pacific	142.3	148.4	151.6	64.7	61.2	56.9
South Asia	425.0	458.8	498.2	91.1	89.1	87.2
Latin America and the Caribbean	67.3	72.4	74.5	35.4	33.6	30.9
Middle East and North Africa	35.8	40.5	42.8	41.3	39.5	34.7
Sub-Saharan Africa	186.3	209.5	235.5	86.5	86.8	86.3

Source: International Labour Office, Global employment trends, Brief, January 2007, p. 11, table 4.

Abbreviations: EU, European Union; CIS, Commonwealth of Independent States.

a/ Preliminary estimates.

compared with 74.0 per cent of men, and in 1996, 49.6 per cent of women were employed, compared with 75.7 per cent of men.

The fact that there is also a gender gap in labour-force participation is another indication that women have limited chances to be a part of the world of paid work. Across all regions, male participation rates dropped from 80.5 per cent in 1996 to 78.8 per cent in 2006. In contrast, 52.4 per cent of all women of working age were either looking for work or working in 2006, a figure that was 0.6 percentage points less than that of 10 years ago. This minimal change in the female participation rate reflects two diverging trends: an increase in prime-age participation and a decrease in youth participation. That latter trend results from the participation of more women in education which should, of course, improve their chances in labour markets.

These global trends should be considered, however, in conjunction with regional diversities.

In 2005, about 84 per cent of the global labour force was found in developing countries, with Asia and the Pacific accounting for about 60 per cent of world employment. China accounted for 26.0 per cent and India for 14.8 per cent of world employment. As the sum of the populations of both countries amounts to over 2 billion people, the increased integration of these two economies into the global trading system provides an abundant labour supply and dampens wage pressure at the global level, at least for the production of tradable goods and services.

There was a decline in unemployment rate in developed economies from 7.8 per cent in 1996 to 6.2 per cent in 2006, which was attributed to strong economic growth coupled with a slower increase in labour-force growth, along with increased labour productivity.

In South-East Asia and the Pacific, the unemployment rate rose significantly, from 3.7 per cent in 1996 to 6.6 per cent in 2006, reflecting in part the lingering impact of the Asian crisis of 1997-1998. In the same period, unemployment in South Asia rose from 4.4 to 5.2 per cent despite growth in gross domestic product (GDP) of 5.8 per cent in 2005.

In Latin America and the Caribbean, the unemployment rate remained at about 8 per cent during the period 1996-2006, despite an annual increase of 2.4 per cent in the total labour force. Economic growth, averaging 3 per cent over the same period, helped to hold down unemployment while lowering the share of the working poor in total employment.

Unemployment in Africa is among the highest in the world. The unemployment rate in sub-Saharan Africa worsened, increasing from 9.2 to 9.8 per cent between 1996 and 2006, even as GDP in the region grew at 3.9 per cent per annum. The Middle East and Northern Africa saw some improvement, with the unemployment rate having declined from 13.0 to 12.2 per cent over the same period. In Africa, unemployment is unevenly distributed across countries, by gender and age groups. Dominated by agriculture, Africa is facing challenges that include low productivity, high demographic growth, worsening youth unemployment, and the massive toll on the labour force taken by HIV/AIDS and the brain drain.

Sectoral changes

In 2006, the employment share of the service sector in total global employment reached 40 per cent and, for the first time, overtook the share of agriculture which was 38.7 per cent. The industry sector accounted for 21.3 per cent of total employment, a figure virtually identical to that of 10 years ago.

Global decline of agricultural labour

Agriculture still accounts for about 45 per cent of the world's labour force, or about 1.3 billion people. In developing countries, about 55 per cent of the labour force is in agriculture, with the figure being close to two thirds in many parts of Africa and Asia. These figures should be treated as rough orders of magnitude, especially since many of those performing agricultural work or labour are also engaged in other forms of non-farm work. Rural employment has been associated with low incomes, and undoubtedly, rural poverty rates are higher than urban ones, particularly in African countries, where a recent modest decline in the difference between rural and urban poverty has been associated with rises in urban poverty levels rather than with any decline in rural poverty (Nkurunziza, 2006, p. 3).

The level of employment in agriculture is extremely small in most developed countries, and has been declining steadily for many generations; on the other hand, it has been declining considerably in developing countries as well.

The fact that, while agricultural output has expanded, in many parts of the world employment in agriculture has shrunk partly reflects efforts to "modernize" farming and to shift to more export-oriented production, often as part of a structural adjustment programme.

There is also strong evidence that the modernization and commercialization of agriculture in developing countries have tended to generate greater inequalities in rural areas, since the primary beneficiaries have been large-scale farmers and agro-industrial corporations, leading to a marginalization of smallholders. This has often been the case in Africa, Central America and Asia (Kwa, 2001).

For many decades, rural livelihoods have been affected by the urban bias of policymakers and politicians, who have tended to favour the interests of the middle class and the elite located mainly in richer urban areas. Peasants and smallholders, as well as landless rural labourers, have had very poor political representation, and thus their work and welfare needs have been severely neglected. However, with the trend towards political democratization, the sheer numbers of potential voters in rural areas might alter this situation.

Indeed, there have been positive developments in recent years. Success has come when policy reforms focused on enhancing the extent of economic security in rural areas, expanding opportunities through land reforms and decentralizing economic decision-making so as to make it more transparent and more answerable to local pressures (see box I.1).

Nonetheless, internationally, smallholder farmers have had their livelihoods adversely affected by the huge food production subsidies provided in the developed countries. These have made it much harder for smallholders to export their produce.[2]

One long-held hope has been that rural living standards could be boosted by the expansion of non-farm rural employment. This was the case in the early stages of economic reform in China during the 1980s, when the rapid growth of township and village enterprises created off-farm employment in rural areas for rural residents, thereby raising rural income. In Africa, where much of the non-farm rural labour is performed by impoverished landless workers, there is relatively little available opportunity to escape from poverty or to obtain sustainable decent work (Demeke, Guta and Ferede, 2003). Non-farm rural labour does seem to offer more decent opportunities in some parts of Latin America and Asia (Gordon and Craig, 2001). However, policies designed to expand non-farm rural employment

Box I.1
Addressing land-related challenges to job creation:
examples of policy responses

Security of tenure

- The rural land plan of Côte d'Ivoire seeks to identify and map all existing rights in order to give them legal status.

- Cameroon's 1974 land ordinance rescinded legal recognition of customary and communal tenure rights and imposed land titling as the only means of acquiring private ownership.

- Uganda's 1995 constitution transfers title from the State directly to landholders.

Conflict management

- The Niger's 1986 rural code seeks to resolve land tenure conflicts.

Decentralization of land administration

- There were established land boards in Botswana (currently in Namibia and Uganda as well), rural councils in Senegal, land commissions in the Niger, community trusts and communal property associations in South Africa and land committees in rural Lesotho. Public participation in decision-making through local institutions was improved.

- Lesotho's 1998 land regulations require land committees to revoke an allocation in the event that the recipient refuses to adopt soil conservation measures.

Land-use development and agricultural productivity

- The Swynnerton Plan of Kenya supported African agriculture through agricultural research programmes, credit schemes, transfer of new technology and introduction of high-value crops and a new set of institutions.

- Ethiopia's agricultural development-led industrialization seeks to increase the productivity of smallholder farmers by dispensing fertilizers and improved seeds, establishing credit schemes and providing support services.

Equitable redistribution to reduce landlessness

- Redistributive land reform policies seek to give more land to landless blacks in Malawi, Namibia, and South Africa.

- Mozambique's 1998 land law recognizes the right to land through occupation by rural families, based on oral testimony.

Development of a land information system

- Kenya's tenure reforms sought to establish a well-maintained registry that could be used to monitor land transfers and distribution.

Source: Nkurunziza (2006), p. 17, table 4.

may not have much potential for lowering poverty or for reducing inequality, since the higher-income activities are typically undertaken by those with other resources and higher incomes (Reardon and others, 1998). This implies that escape from poverty is critically dependent on secure access to resources, including income, assets, skills, transport, energy and network connections.

There is also a debate being held in Africa in particular, on the merits of policies designed to enhance the capacity of rural-dwellers to remain independent smallholders versus those aimed at accelerating the trend towards greater wage employment. According to one argument, the shift to wage labour is associated with rising labour productivity and thus with higher rural earnings. Yet, there is evidence that rural wage labour is usually precarious and leaves rural workers more exposed to exploitation and onerous working conditions. In between lie various forms of production cooperative, long regarded as a desirable and viable form of the agrarian productive system and a means to expand productive employment. The fair trade movement, a trading partnership particularly relevant to agricultural cooperatives, is one of the initiatives trying to strengthen this mechanism.

Deindustrialization

One phenomenon that has been linked to relatively high unemployment and employment restructuring in developed countries is "deindustrialization", whereby manufacturing jobs are shed by those countries while manufacturing output expands. This tendency had developed in the United Kingdom of Great Britain and Northern Ireland as early as the 1980s. Since then, it has been shown to be characteristic of all developed countries led by the United States of America, where the disappearance of manufacturing jobs has been truly remarkable. The United States "lost" 3.5 million manufacturing jobs between 1998 and 2005 alone.

In developing countries, there has been both deindustrialization and some industrialization: deindustrialization to the extent that growth of industrial output has been expanding without generating a similar rate of manufacturing employment growth, owing to labour-market liberalization and other structural adjustment measures; and some industrialization, to the extent that industrial output and exports are growing as a share of GDP. What is perhaps unique is that output growth is not strongly related to employment growth.

Deindustrialization in terms of employment has been occurring in many developing countries, including the two rapidly growing economies that have been successful in expanding their shares of world trade in manufacturing products, namely, China and India. Such deindustrialization is characterized by a net transfer of jobs from agriculture to services, many of which are low-paying and precarious and are not covered by formal mechanisms of social protection. This has been particularly the case in many Asian countries.

The world is rapidly becoming an economic system dominated by the service sector, in which mean average productivity and income levels are low. At the same time, there is a high degree of income inequality, largely owing to the presence of a minority engaged in very highly paid professional and personal services and finance.

Jobless growth

As mentioned earlier in this chapter, many countries, as well as the world as a whole, seem to be suffering from "jobless growth". In other words, their economy is growing without any jobs having been generated, or the number of jobs created has been diminishing for any given rate of economic growth.

Why is employment inversely related to economic growth, particularly in South-East Asian economies? What is behind the stories of jobless growth? According to one interpretation, this is a restructuring phenomenon that will last a few years until such time as labour productivity has risen to world levels, after which employment will grow more rapidly. According to another, complementary interpretation in actual fact industrial employment has risen but much of it is indirect, through subcontracting and the use of casual, flexible labour that is not picked up in employment statistics.

Several variants of the latter view have emerged. One is related to the idea of restructuring unemployment. In the United States, for example, a popular view is that recent recessions have resulted in proportionately more permanent losses of jobs relative to the number of layoffs than was the case up to the 1980s (Groshen and Potter, 2003). When a recovery takes place, those who were made redundant, instead of being recalled to their old jobs or even to similar jobs in the industry in which they had been working, must find jobs in other sectors. The result is that employment recovers more slowly than output, inasmuch as it takes more time for workers to move into alternative employment.

More generally, when growth picks up, firms take the opportunity to introduce higher-technology machinery and equipment, thereby reducing the labour-capital ratio and making extra employment unnecessary, and are even induced to cut their workforces. While this represents a boost to productivity, which is an essential requirement for long-term growth and development, the problem is that workers are not gaining proportionately from this productivity growth.

Another view is that jobless growth has as much to do with the changes in the types of labour relationships occurring in the wake of the pursuit of labour-market flexibility. It is easier for employers to conceal the existence of many of the workers with non-regular work status, with the result that they do not appear in the employment statistics. Thus, the phenomenon of jobless growth may be, to some extent at least, a deceptive one. Employers around the world are known to agree to pay workers more than they would otherwise be paid if they can keep them off the books.

Regardless of the possible reasons for jobless growth, the phenomenon is an unwelcome one in the context of decent work. Whether technological changes are raising productivity without benefiting workers, or structural adjustment is causing workers to have to find employment in other sectors, or more flexible/casual employment situations are not registering in traditional labour statistics, the outcome of the process is the same: workers are losing wages and/or job security.

Global informalization

There has been an informalization of employment and work in many parts of the world. In contrast with past experience, economic growth has not been strongly associated with the growth of formal employment; indeed, informal activities, however defined, seem to have grown in absolute and in relative terms.

According to the International Labour Office (2002a), between 50 and 70 per cent of workers in developing countries are in informal work. In some countries, the figure is even higher. Most are in some form of "self-employment", although a large number are in casual jobs. Most are engaged in low-productivity petty production in unregistered firms or businesses.

In Latin America, the importance of what many still call the informal sector as a source of new jobs is unmistakable. By 2000, this "sector" was providing about 47 per cent of total urban employment (Tokman, 2006). Moreover, its share in the labour market has continued to grow steadily. Out of every 100 jobs created since 1980, about 70 have been informal in character; indeed, with respect to non-agricultural employment, the proportion of informal workers in urban employment grew from 40 per cent in 1980 to more than half at present.

The growing informality of Latin American employment has also been undergoing a transformation, in that microenterprises (having less than five workers) are showing the highest rate of growth. An increasing number of such enterprises are becoming a valid job-creation option with respect to income, although they are still far from offering acceptable conditions in terms of job stability and social protection.

Recently, changes in labour laws in many parts of Latin America have made it easier for enterprises to hire workers under atypical, generally fixed-term contracts characterized by precariousness, either because of built-in occupational instability, or owing to a legal or de facto reduction of the levels of social and labour protection. Thus, undeclared and precarious labour, usually associated with informality, has been building up in the labour market. Informality, illegality and precariousness have become almost synonymous.

So far, the analysis has treated economic activity as either formal or informal; dichotomies are not as helpful as the more nuanced concept of a continuum of degrees of informality (International Labour Office, 2004a). Decent work lies in having some informality, but with security safeguards. There is a temptation to idealize formal employment and to regard the increase in the size of informal employment as a wholly negative phenomenon. Yet, many people all over the world welcome the informality of flexible working time, varied tasks and the greater autonomy connected with work that is not characteristic of formal jobs. The trouble is that informal employment, to the extent that it may be low-income, precarious and lacking in protection, has been equated with "bad" employment.

In general, there are solid reasons for believing that as a result of globalization and the global trend towards more flexible labour-market relations, many forms of labour are becoming more rather than less informal; but it is crucial to see this as a combination of changes of the type illustrated in box I.2.

There appears to be widespread agreement regarding certain trends. For example, the level of informalized labour and work seems to rise during and after economic shocks. To some extent, this may be a sectoral effect, involving a loss of jobs in wage-earning employment, but it may also reflect an alteration in the structure of work status within those sectors hit by the shock, as firms take advantage of the situation to outsource and subcontract, rather than rely on direct employment.

Box I.2
Labour informality trends

People who are in income-earning activity have widely differing levels of informality. Some are in highly regulated employment, with social protection and access to a wide range of benefits; and some have little or no protection and lack any viable form of contract.

We may define formality as encompassing a spectrum, depending on work status, workplace type, access to employment protection, contract status and regularity of employment. In doing so, we can generate a simple continuum ranging workers by extent of formality or informality simply by summing the score on each of the five measures. While this is very approximate, it highlights the reality of a wide range of statuses and work situations.

For example, data from a survey carried out in Gujarat, India, in 2000 show that while most men and women workers are in highly informal forms of employment, many (about 20 per cent) are in employment that is neither very informal nor very formal.

If we apply the same methodology to very similar data from a comparable survey in China, we find that the continuum generated is almost a mirror image. There is evidence, however, that the shape of the continuum is changing, so that more members of the workforce are shifting towards forms of employment that are represented by the columns on the left-hand side of the figure, that is to say, workers are becoming more informalized.

Degree of employment informality by sex, Gujarat, India

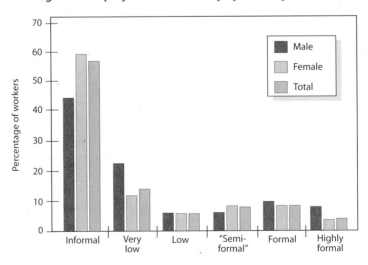

Source: International Labour Office (2004a).

It is important to establish what actually happens in such cases. If what happens is that employers are shifting to the use of more flexible labour relationships, the perception of the informal economy as a survival zone of poverty, insecurity and chronic underemployment may not be accurate. In this case, shocks, rather than legislative or regulatory reforms, become a way of liberalizing labour markets.

Informalization is closely linked to labour casualization. Labour-market restructuring, often creating greater flexibility in the labour market, has increasingly led to the spread of precarious labour relationships, especially employment insecurity, which manifests itself in various forms. Globally, there has been a spread of short-term contracts, giving workers few entitlements and little sense of permanence in their employment. Extensive casualization has always characterized labour relationships in developing countries, but it has been growing elsewhere as well. Often, workers retain short-term status even though they have remained in their jobs for many years. The fact that these workers face constant insecurity makes them less inclined to object to workplace changes, to wage cuts or to loss of benefits out of fear of losing their jobs.

Besides the direct shift to casual work, a significant development has been the growth of agency labour, hired out by private employment agencies to firms for short-term work assignments. Often, the agency becomes the actual employer and in such cases, there may be non-wage benefits provided, such as entitlement to medical insurance or sick pay, but the worker has no attachment to a particular enterprise or company. Moving workers around from workplace to workplace undermines any sense of collective bonding and thus acts to weaken workforces in their bargaining with employers. In sum, there is a tendency for corporations to build some casualization into their employment structures, and to promote, rather than prevent, high labour turnover, thereby limiting the extent of high seniority pay and entrenched non-wage benefits.

Unemployment and labour-market insecurity

In many countries, it has been almost impossible to estimate open unemployment at all; and in those cases, it is unhelpful to equate low unemployment with full employment. The emergence of open unemployment reflects the existence of unemployment benefits and employment services and the erosion of family-based or community-based systems of social support in times of economic need.

The key point is that an increase in open unemployment does not necessarily mean that there has been a deterioration of the labour market or that there has been a move away from full employment.

Open unemployment may also emerge or rise as a result of a beneficial shift of production and employment from low-productivity to higher-productivity sectors. In such circumstances, what was underemployment becomes open unemployment. This is particularly relevant in the case of economic shocks, since they usually induce some restructuring, often from rural, domestically-oriented production to urban, export-oriented growth. In such cases, open measured unemployment could rise, while underemployment could fall.

At the same time, shocks could induce job-shedding and firm-restructuring designed to raise long-term productivity growth. Something like this may have happened in the wake of several of the Latin American economic crises of recent years, where open unemployment remained high years after economic growth had recovered (see figure I.2).

Of particular concern, is the issue of long-term unemployment, that is to say, situations in which workers are looking for income-earning work for periods of more than a year. This type of prolonged unemployment is often taken to represent unemployment in general. Although this is not the case, such a situation is the one with which impoverishment is most associated, entailing, as it does, a gradual loss of networks of support, a loss of energy and willpower, and debilitation.

Concern about the extent and seriousness of long-term unemployment is especially prominent in Europe, having led to proposals for active labour-market policy in order to ensure the social integration of the jobless. A belief that the long-term unemployed lose the will to work has led politicians to favour more stringent policies, to take away benefits or to restrict the duration of entitlement, as well as to require that the long-term unemployed take jobs or undertake training.

In middle-income developing countries, there are few data on the extent of long-term unemployment. Given the lack of unemployment benefits and the need for those affected to do almost anything in order to survive, it is to be expected that many of the unemployed will drift into informal activities and underemployment. Many who stay without work for an extended period probably become "unemployable".

Figure I.2.
Medium-term effects of financial crises on
unemployment in Latin American countries, 1991-2002

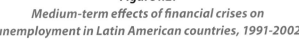

Argentina (financial crisis in 1995 and 2001-2002)

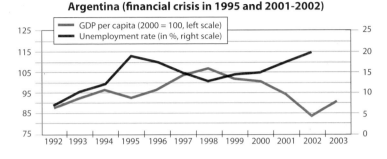

Brazil (financial crisis in 1998-1999)

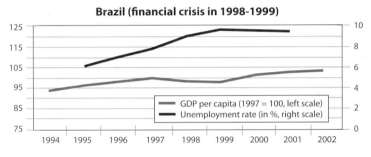

Chile (financial crisis in 1998-1999)

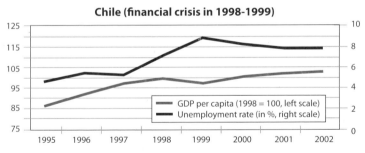

Mexico (financial crisis in 1994-1995)

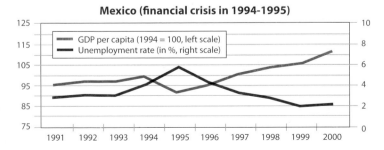

Source: van der Hoeven and Lubker (2006), p. 13, graph 5.

The occurrence of prolonged recessions in some countries is particularly pernicious, as it creates a disproportionate growth of long-term unemployment. This is almost certainly the case in developing countries, where consequently a large segment of the working-age population are being marginalized and, in the absence of corrective measures, are being cut off from the mainstream labour-market permanently.

What this means is that whether or not national economies recover from a financial crisis or economic or social shock — all of which are becoming more common — the longer-term adverse effects on workers at the margins of the labour market may be permanent. This tendency has major implications for the design and structure of social policy interventions. Ironically, in the aftermath of economic shocks, open unemployment may not stay high because many of the longer-term unemployed fall into a state of discouragement, cease searching for jobs, and become disabled or ill to the point where they no longer count in the labour force.

Outsourcing or offshoring

While the global transformation is involving a major movement of people, mostly in search of income-earning work, there also exists a migration of jobs. One of the most controversial aspects of globalization is the perception that corporations in developed countries are transferring jobs to lower-income, labour-surplus countries. This is commonly called offshoring or outsourcing, although, actually, there are several forms, namely, insourcing offshoring, whereby a multinational corporation shifts its production (and employment) to its own plants elsewhere; outsourcing offshoring, whereby companies transfer production and employment to quasi-independent suppliers, and outsourcing inshoring, whereby multinational companies hire independent suppliers at home instead of shifting production to their overseas plants.

In sum, offshoring and outsourcing of jobs are poorly monitored and surveyed. They are surely underestimated in the sense that transfers of jobs take place mostly at the margin, through boardroom decisions or through steady adjustments in the direction of investments. To some extent, the actual numbers claimed are only a part of the emerging challenge. It is the *ex ante* anticipation of possible shifts that engenders fear and insecurity among workers, which in turn renders them more amenable to making concessions in the workplace, such as accepting lower pay, accepting and the loss of long-entrenched benefits.

The very fact that firms can offshore and outsource alters the balance of bargaining power of workers and employers. It puts the onus on all concerned in respect of finding ways to make labour more dignifying and to discourage "free riders", or those who may benefit in the short term by offering lower wages or benefits, amid worsening working conditions.

Working time

Another aspect of globalization and labour-market liberalization is their impact on the level and distribution of working time. Undoubtedly, there has been a rise in female labour-force participation all over the world, which is partly due to the spread of more flexible forms of labour; but to some extent, this has been associated with changes in the pattern of labour-force participation more generally. There has been a growth in more intermittent labour-force participation, with more people remaining for certain periods outside of the labour market, and some taking what amounts to sabbaticals.

The growth of part-time labour has been a part of this process, particularly among the youth still pursuing some form of schooling and among older workers, more of whom wish to remain in the labour market or are forced to do so because they have no pension or only a modest one. This has been fostered by employment opportunities in the service sector in many parts of the world economy, since part-time and intermittent labour are more common in services than in manufacturing. However, there is also evidence that it is harder to regulate working time in services, with the result that there is concern that more people are working very long days and weeks. Indeed, a recent ILO study by Lee, McCann and Messenger (2007) estimated that 614.2 million workers, making up 22.0 per cent of the global workforce, are working more than 48 hours per week. In addition, there are also concerns about more people being on call, and having to be available to work on short notice without the security that comes with negotiated standard working times.

In a liberalized global economic system, what is practised in one major economy puts pressure on other countries to allow similar practices in the interest of "competitiveness". Employers and Governments want to allow adjustments in working time to meet fluctuating demand, and thereby lower their labour and production costs. The fact that this has led many to make their employment more flexible imposes more uncertainty on workers.

Concluding remarks

The world of work is being profoundly transformed. Sectoral shifts are themselves making the old images of full-time, single-occupation labour and employment inappropriate as guides to the future.

Above all, the sense of insecurity accompanying the different forms of "informality" and the lack of employment security pose major challenges for the twenty-first century. It is not just the precariousness of labour and work that poses this challenge, but the shift towards flexible living including migration for work and other purposes which will figure ever more prominently in a more truly global economy and society.

In recent years, employment-promotion has taken on renewed prominence in policymaking. Employment-generation is increasingly seen as essential for reducing poverty. However, given the nature of emerging labour markets and the tendency for many more jobs to generate low incomes, this view promises to be the fulcrum of major policy debates in the next few years.

With global deindustrialization, greater labour informality and flexibility and a rapidly evolving internationalized labour system, policymakers may need to shift to novel and quite different ways of thinking if they are going to promote an environment in which decent work and employment can flourish in conditions of freedom and economic security. In particular, they will need to consider how to reform systems of social protection to enable them to meet the challenge of an era of increased labour-market flexibility. For a future of decent work, more equitable systems of regulation and of social protection and redistribution are required, at subnational, national, regional and global levels.

Notes

[1] Employment-related terms used in the present report were taken from the International Labour Office (ILO) and are defined as follows: The labour-force participation rate is a measure of the proportion of a country's working-age population that engages actively in the labour market, by either working or looking for work. The expression in work encompasses all people employed according to the ILO definition, which includes the self-employed, the employed, and employers as well as unpaid family members. The unemployment rate refers to the proportion of the labour force that does not have a job and is actively looking for work. The working poor are those employed persons who are unable to generate sufficient income from their labour to maintain a minimum standard of living and who are estimated to be below the poverty line. (In this case, the poverty line refers to the levels of both US$ 1 per person per day and US$ 2 per person per day). More information is available from *http://www.ilo.org/public/english/ employment/strat/kilm/indicators.htm#kilm2.*

[2] Recently, a fair trade movement has emerged, through which agricultural goods produced by smallholders in developing countries have been guaranteed a "fair price" in developed countries. Under fair trade, cooperative producers or democratic organizations in developing countries partner with distributors and consumer groups in developed countries. Producers are paid a price guaranteed to at least cover the costs of production while meeting international labour standards and non-discriminatory practices. The fair price guarantee enables producer cooperatives to be viable and to compete in an imperfect global market. One product in respect of which fair trade has been most successful is coffee. An increasing number of cooperative coffee growers in Ghana, Ethiopia and the United Republic of Tanzania are participating in fair trade arrangements and reaping the benefits of fair pricing.

Chapter II

The impact of global economic and social liberalization

The current era of globalization has been defined by as the systematic spread of capital and open markets, by fewer constraints imposed by institutions or regulatory interventions and consequently by increasingly internationally integrated markets. The long-term trend is supposed to be fully open markets for goods and services, capital, technology and labour. However, a fully global market for labour has been the slowest to emerge, despite greater labour-market flexibility at the national level.

This globalization process has been accompanied and reinforced by social and economic reforms in countries all over the world. The key aspects of these reforms over the past three decades, insofar as they have a bearing on employment and the labour market, are the liberalization of goods and services markets, economic privatization, the deregulation and commercialization of social services and social protection, the strengthening of poverty reduction strategies, labour-market re-regulation and labour contracting, whereby more workers and employees are hired through intermediaries or have individual written employment contracts setting out personal conditions, entitlements and expectations, instead of standard or collective contracts.

Liberalization, commercialization and economic volatility

The impacts of these trends on the situation of employment and work are twofold. Some of these changes have direct consequences for the conditions and terms of employment and work, while others affect employment and work indirectly through the performance of the economy. Both the direct and indirect effects need to be examined in order to fully understand the extent to which employment and work have evolved in the twenty-first century.

Trade liberalization

The rate of growth of trade (exports and imports) has long been much greater than the rate of growth of gross domestic product (GDP). This has affected the structure of production and employment in developing countries to a very considerable extent, especially since the shift in recent decades from "import substitution" and food security to "export-orientation".

Trade liberalization alone, however, does not lead to higher economic growth unless other policies, such as those that encourage investment, allow effective conflict resolution and promote human resources development, are introduced at the same time (Winters, 2004; World Bank, 2005a). Recent evidence suggests that only in exceptional circumstances, does trade liberalization seem to boost growth and employment. What it also seems to do is increase income inequality and wage differentials (see, for example, Lee (2005)).

One aspect of trade liberalization that has had a rather dramatic effect in recent times was termination on 1 January 2005 of the Agreement on Textiles and Clothing, which largely removed quantitative quota restrictions. This had an immediate effect on the international structure of apparel and clothing exports and imports. Since developing countries accounted for more than half of the world's exports of those products at the time (World Trade Organization (2006)), this change had a major effect on those countries.

Liberalization of trade in clothing and textiles would appear to offer advantages to developing countries because they are deemed to have a comparative advantage in those sectors, which traditionally rely on manual labour. However, the disruptive effects on production and labour markets of the termination of the Agreement on Textiles and Clothing were considerable, and different developing countries were affected in different ways. Indeed, trade and production patterns changed dramatically while total trade grew in 2005 and 2006. A few countries benefited, while sharp losses of jobs occurred in other countries, some of which had relied on making garments to a much greater extent than those that benefited from the termination of the Agreement.

Finally, as far as trade liberalization is concerned, policymakers need to assess the impact of the growing number of bilateral arrangements. A concern is that bilateral trade agreements might reflect the relative bargaining strength of the respective countries, thus imposing more onerous terms on the weaker party. In particular, such agreements might impose conditions that could impede a country's ability to pursue domestic employment and social policies that would be welfare-enhancing. It is for this reason, among others, that many believe that a multilateral framework is inherently superior to a mishmash of bilateral agreements.

Financial market liberalization

Although trade liberalization has probably received most attention, financial liberalization, including capital-account liberalization, has caused most concern in recent years. Financial market liberalization has led to financial integration, which clearly has imposed limitations on the autonomous capacity of national policy-makers to shape their policies and control the extent of macroeconomic stability. The inability to operate counter-cyclical fiscal and monetary policy means inter alia, that recessions are more likely to be deep and prolonged; and for this reason alone, such recessions are likely to lead to more long-term unemployment.

Integration has also meant that movements on one national market are more closely linked to movements in financial markets elsewhere, resulting in greater market volatility. It has also intensified bank competition and increased the focus on short-term investments relative to longer-term investments (Williamson, 2002). All of these aspects of financial integration have imparted a greater degree of market volatility, which translates into greater volatility in national economies and labour markets, particularly in smaller countries.

Advocates of liberalization have long argued that financial market liberalization in itself would boost economic growth and lead to more stable growth, as well as a convergence in living standards between countries. These strong claims have been highly controversial and, as indicated in the next section, there are reasons for scepticism. After having advocated liberalization, even the World Bank (2005a), in reviewing growth performance of developing countries in the 1990s, concluded that: "Contrary to expectations, financial liberalization did not add much to growth, and it appears to have augmented the number of crises" (p. 21).

Greater economic volatility leads to greater income and employment insecurity. A crucial social policy point is that the growing tendency for shocks and economic volatility to arise means that conventional social insurance and contingency benefit schemes are made weaker, since whole communities are hit by adverse events, rather than a few individuals at a time. This situation leaves traditional social security schemes under intense pressure and traditional informal networks of support unable to cope.

Foreign direct investment

Even in the case of actual foreign productive investment, foreign direct investment (FDI) has engendered more national economic insecurity, since increasingly capital can be switched between countries relatively easily. Indeed, FDI has been part of a trend towards multinationalization of production, whereby corporations with numerous subsidiaries can switch production and thus employment from one location to another quickly and at little cost.

This enhanced flexibility gives them a stronger bargaining position with national Governments and with workers as well as trade unions bargaining on their behalf. In effect, the character of globalized FDI has been changing, and instead of a central base linked to subsidiaries, there is a more globally integrated production system, which has effects on labour and employment practices.

The (International Labour Office, 2004b, para. 35) has argued that in developing countries, the employment effects of FDI have been "rather weak" and that:

> At the same time, a rising share of FDI in total investment tends to reduce the overall employment elasticity while shifting the pattern of labour demand in favour of high-skilled labour. Rising wage inequality is also a consequence. On the positive side, a rising share of FDI in total investment leads to an improvement in the average quality of employment for both high-skilled and low-skilled labour.

Others have argued that FDI makes the demand for labour more sensitive with respect to changes in prices and growth, meaning that the growth of FDI has increased the volatility of employment and earnings, thus making for greater economic insecurity among workers and local communities (Slaughter, 2001; Görg and Strobl, 2003). Indeed, some have concluded that multinationals pay higher wages than local firms in part to compensate workers for the greater employment volatility (Sheve and Slaughter, 2002), as multinational plants are more likely to close in response to economic downturns (Bernard and Jensen, 2002).

In sum, FDI and the global integration of production have become a driving force of the global economy, and appear set to determine the nature of labour markets and foster the tendency towards a global convergence of labour and employment practices, for better or for worse.

Fiscal policy reform

Fiscal prudence has been the watchword in the past decades. In reality this implied a requirement that Governments slash social spending to levels not exceeding fiscal revenues. At the same time, revenues were reduced by tax cuts intended to create incentives. In particular, developing countries have been obliged to cut import taxes, owing to trade liberalization and multilateral trade rules. This has impeded their social and other public spending by which they could have boosted growth and employment. Health-care spending particularly has suffered (United Nations Conference on Trade and Development, 2006). Severe health problems facing many developing countries have impaired the productive capacities of workers and made it correspondingly harder to boost employment.

More generally, there has been a steady shift away from taxation of capital towards greater taxation of labour. Country after country has cut tax rates on capital. At the same time, there has been a shift in the direction of fiscal subsidies: subsidies to capital have gone up sharply and steadily while those to labour have declined and consumer subsidies in particular have been whittled away in the name of removing market distortions. This double shift in fiscal policy obviously has a regressive effect on overall income distribution. It also affects the demand for labour, as the relative prices of capital and labour are affected, and thus the level of employment.

Cutting social spending that could have boosted employment growth is only one element of fiscal reforms that have had adverse effect on employment and labour. Indeed, the changing level and distribution of subsidies have constituted one of the most striking features of the globalization era, involving annual payments worth about 4 per cent of global GDP (van Beers and de Moor, 2001).

Governments provide subsidies for many reasons (World Trade Organization, 2006). The most laudable is to ensure universal access to services and infrastructure and to take account of externalities. However, very often subsidies are designed to favour strategic sectors, or to boost exports or limit imports, or to limit job losses or assist in job-generation. These are the sorts of reasons that generate criticism of subsidies. Sometimes, subsidies involve deadweight effects, that is to say, they are given to firms for doing something that they would have done anyway. Often, subsidies also involve large substitution effects, that is to say, they enable one firm or sector to displace another, whether or not that is the intention.

Although subsidies are now often needed to develop new productive and export capacities, employment opportunities or greater productivity, they are difficult to sustain and involve trade-offs with alternative public spending choices. They are also likely to be abused and typically go to socio-economic interests that have a relatively strong political bargaining position, inside the country and/or outside it. When observers claim that Governments cannot afford the public social spending that would overcome the economic insecurity of the disadvantaged, they should look closely at the extent and *distribution* of subsidies provided by the State.

Social service liberalization

The recent deregulation, privatization and marketization of social services have had a profound effect on labour markets in sectors of employment that had set standards of social security for several generations. Several trends have emerged. There has been increasing commercialization of service provision, entailing larger payments by users and the greater centralization of pricing and profitability decisions. There has also been a trend towards decentralization of services, with responsibility devolved to local authorities though not necessarily contracted out to private commercial providers. Moreover, the progress of the processes of privatization has been uneven, with formerly public services being sold off to private commercial providers, and Governments creating openings for private firms so they can provide such services.

The transformation of social services — health, education, employment services, pensions, care, social services, prisons, water, gas, electricity and so on — has been a crucial aspect of the transformation of labour and work across the world. There have been many consequences. For example:

(a) Workers providing social services have tended to experience a reduction in employment security and income security, and to lose representation, since private sector workers are much less likely to be unionized or to have the workplace safeguards that have been the norm in the public sector. Liberalization and privatization have meant that "permanent" employment, characteristic of civil services until a few years ago, is diminishing rapidly. Many more workers have been placed on short-term contracts, with periods of short notice for dismissal. Outsourcing and subcontracting have become far more common, so that more workers in the service sector are receiving incomes that reflect specific demand, and thus experience more fluctuations in their earnings. All these changes may have helped to reduce labour costs, but at the cost of creating many more insecurities for those providing the services;

(b) Commercialization, decentralization and privatization have tended to produce greater differentiation among occupational groups within specific services in terms of wages, benefits, job security, employment security, work safety and representation (Rosskam, 2006);

(c) Those using the services have also been affected in several ways, primarily because the more fortunate, those with the ability to pay, have benefited from greater "choice" and from the higher-quality services on offer to those who can pay. This has, inter alia, freed up more of their time for work and leisure activities, while those with little ability to pay have had not only to pay a larger proportion of their income (and often, a larger premium for some services, owing to their lower insurability), but also to use up more of their time and energy in order to obtain the service. In effect, the poor pay for the service with income and their work time, while the rich pay only with their income.

Example (c) has received insufficient attention. For instance, if schooling or medical services are provided on a private commercial basis, those able to pay can obtain priority treatment, avoiding queues and being less likely to travel long distances to obtain the service. Those who are poor tend to have to walk long distances, join long queues and pay higher premiums for insurance and they are often forced by financial circumstances to try to rely on a run-down public service.

Advocates of the commercialization, decentralization and privatization of social services claim that these promote greater efficiency, which they believe will eventually benefit whole societies. This may be correct. However, it is fairly clear that various forms of inequality have widened, affecting in the process the character of the work of those providing the services and the work situation of many of the groups receiving them (United Nations, 2005a).

Labour-market flexibility

The three main forms of flexibility are considered to be external/internal (or functional) flexibility, working time flexibility and wage flexibility. Critics of many welfare State labour markets contend that these markets are made inflexible by the existence of institutional distortions, which prevent greater employment. Labour regulations, trade unions, collective bargaining and statutory minimum wages have been identified as the main sources of labour-market inflexibility.

External flexibility is high if workers can and do move rapidly and relatively costlessly from sectors or occupations experiencing declining demand to those that are expanding. The claim is that barriers, usually including employment protection legislation, prevent employers from cutting their employment in times of shrinking demand, thus imposing higher labour costs and impeding their productivity and profitability, and in the longer term, preventing them from being sustainable enterprises. They also claim that such barriers cause employers to opt for more capital-intensive technologies than might otherwise be the case, and deter them from hiring because of a fear of a downturn that would leave them with high fixed labour costs.

Many have challenged this argument maintaining, for instance, that employment protection boosts long-term commitment and labour productivity and induces employers to plan their employment more carefully. The evidence is mixed. What is clear, however, is that in their effort to remain or become economically competitive, Governments and employers around the world have taken numerous steps to increase external labour-market flexibility, and in doing so have imposed greater labour-related insecurity on most groups of workers.

Moreover, it has not often been asked whether or not an economy can have too great a degree of flexibility. An extremely flexible system is likely to be a highly unstable one, and adjustment costs associated with unstable systems are high, rendering them less efficient than systems where resources are utilized for productive purposes. Above all, the global trend towards employment flexibility means that fewer workers can expect to be engaged in stable protected employment.

Labour-market re-regulation

Contrary to common belief, systematic labour-market re-regulation, as part of a global restructuring of regulations and regulatory institutions, has taken place. Some researchers have focused on non-statutory and "indirect" regulation (see, for example, Arup and others, 2006), while others have concluded that the primary objective of the changes has been to increase as part of the thrust towards more labour market flexibility, the degree to which labour is treated as a commodity, (Standing, 2006). In other words, the intention has been to limit or remove the factors that prevent wages from adjusting so that demand equals supply. This has led to a curbing of the "power" of trade unions through legislation limiting the right to strike and, in some cases, the right to form some types of union. It has included a strengthening of individual protection in some respects while weakening the protection of collective rights.

While the reform process has been uneven around the world, most countries were moving in the same direction until fairly recently. In this regard, it is probably fair to conclude that the role of statutory protective regulations has been diminishing, while greater emphasis has been placed on the following three forms of regulation:

(a)   Self-regulation, through the promotion of "voluntary codes of conduct" and "corporate social responsibility" schemes;

(b)   Fiscal regulation, that is to say, the use of taxes, tax credits and subsidies to guide labour-market behaviour, and to provide incentives for some types of action and penalties for others towards which there has been a steady shift;

(c)   Privatized regulation, that is to say, regulation that fosters a growing role for private, commercial organizations in exerting regulatory pressure on firms, local authorities and Governments as a means of determining their labour and social practices and policies.

Although it has been the least analysed, this last trend raises important questions about the legitimacy of having non-accountable commercial entities shaping labour practices. In particular, in the context of globalization, powerful multinational institutions such as credit rating agencies are increasingly able to influence labour practices and social policies by judging which are good and which are bad.

No doubt one could argue that the credit rating agencies are operating as a market mechanism to promote best practices, but many observers suggest that they have gained quasi-regulatory powers, are generating "adaptation pressure" that are neither accountable nor democratic, and are rather untransparent. They are a means by which national autonomy and even corporate autonomy are being curtailed.

Contractualization and individualization

Globally, there has been a spread of short-term contracts, giving workers few entitlements and little sense of permanence in their employment. Extensive casualization has always characterized labour relationships in developing countries, where workers in large informal sectors often do not have any contract at all, but it has been growing in developed countries as well. For example, a significant development in developed countries in recent years has been the growth of agency labour, whereby private employment agencies hire out workers to firms for short-term assignments. Often workers retain short-term status even though they may have remained in their jobs for many years.

The development of an international labour market in recent years has also been linked to the trend towards more individualized labour contracts. Globally, the implications for employment services and for regulations are considerable.

Standardized contracts and collective contracts are giving way to more individualized contracts based on individual bargaining between employers and workers. One concern is that as the bargaining strengths of managers and individual workers differ enormously, a shift to more decentralized and individualized employment relations would tilt the balance in favour of employers.

Indeed, given the nebulous nature of many casual agreements involving work performed by one person for another, there is a belief that such relationships should be solidified as legal employment, entailing the entitlements, legal protection and obligations that come with such legal status. The tendency for more people to be in a nebulous work status intensified the international pressure that led the International Labour Conference to adopt a new standard, at its 95th session in June 2006, proposing that Governments adopt policies to ensure protection of workers' entitlements, distinguishing between employment and self-employment, while recognizing contractual responsibilities on both sides. This is important in that, in many countries, without an accepted employment relationship, workers cannot procure entitlement to social security or labour protection.

Ironically, with of the ongoing shift towards individual employment contracts in some economies a growing number of workers may find themselves without any contractual protection, to their considerable disadvantage. In contrast, under almost any system of collective bargaining, workers who do not have a specific agreement with an employer are nevertheless usually covered, whether by a system of judicial awards or by sectoral agreements.

The decline of collective bargaining may mean that more workers will have no contract worthy of the name. Instead, the market will rule. This need not happen, but it is a current reality to which policy responses will be required.

Migration

The global movement in recent decades towards greater social and economic deregulation and liberalization has also helped to facilitate migration both within countries and internationally. Most migration is intended to better the life prospects and welfare of those who move. In that context, it remains a challenge for those promoting societies of decent work to facilitate the process and to reduce the costs and increase the benefits of movement both for the migrants and their families, and for communities and labour markets. In this regard, it is important to consider the main forms of movement.

Perhaps rural-urban migration, much of which is seasonal and circular, is still the most substantial form. Several concerns stand out. First, those who leave rural areas tend to be the young, relatively educated and potentially most productive. In some parts of the world, their departure has led to ageing rural labour forces and a consequent decline in productivity and production. Second, there is a tendency for the more successful among such migrants to accentuate the extent of inequality and differentiation in the rural areas by sending back remittances that are used to buy up land or other resources from those in debt or under economic duress. Third, rural migrants tend to be relatively exploitable in urban industrial areas without social networks to support them or knowledge of what wages and benefits they should receive, and with all the fears that accompany being in unfamiliar circumstances.

Another, more particular form of labour migration has been from rural areas into export processing zones, much of it involving young women. Although much has been written about this phenomenon, it deserves to be highlighted, in part because the institutional safeguards for workers in such zones have often been weaker than elsewhere. Often, trade unions have been banned or their activity has been severely curtailed and labour inspections have been less common in the interest of encouraging FDI. In effect, Governments have been deliberately fostering a dualistic labour market as well as a dualistic economy. In these circumstances, migrants, most of whom are short-term, have been especially vulnerable, and there is considerable evidence that they have been treated as a disposable labour reserve, employed for short periods and then laid off when illness or even disability makes them less productive.

A third important form of migration is that of rural young people emigrating to work abroad for short periods, which may stretch into several years. Usually, this has involved young men who go abroad to take jobs as labourers or in mines, and young women who go as maids, as caregivers for children or, intentionally or not, as sex workers. Human trafficking is only one of grave consequences of this form of migration, which has affected millions of people in recent years and almost certainly constitutes one aspect of globalization.

Often, forms of bonded labour and debt bondage have been involved, in which debts are first incurred in rural areas when families pay labour middlemen or agents to assist in the acquisition of job contracts or to ensure transport. In some countries, the resultant indebtedness has led to land dispossession and impoverishment, often because the promised jobs did not materialize, or because the young emigrants were dismissed from their jobs or not paid.

A fourth form of migration, which is more benign in origin and, for the migrants, often beneficial in effect, is represented by the much-discussed phenomenon of brain drain, whereby mostly young and newly educated urban-dwellers move abroad to obtain higher-paying employment than they could obtain in their home countries. By most accounts, this movement has become much greater in the globalization era; and whereas developed countries have tended to erect more barriers against the migration of so-called unskilled workers, they have tended to facilitate the influx of educated skilled professionals.

The movement of students, many of whom combine studying with employment in the country of their studies, that is less well monitored than some others constitutes a form of international migration. Some countries have restricted such employment, but as the market for students has developed, Governments have tended to relax the restrictions, while trying to ensure that they do not substitute for local workers by regulating the extent of the employment that they are allowed to take. The emerging norm seems to be an upper limit of 20 hours per week during term time, with restrictions on the duration of any particular job. Thus, students are becoming a new source of flexible low-wage labour. They tend not to appear in any official statistics either as workers or as labour migrants.

In general, international labour migration, one of the defining features of the globalization era has been substantial and is growing, although the pace may have slowed in the last few years as receiving-country Governments have raised barriers to immigration. In 2005, according to estimates of the United Nations (2006a), there were 191 million migrants living outside their country of origin or citizenship, including those migrating for employment, their dependants, and refugees and asylum–seekers. This was more than double the figure of 82 million recorded in 1970.

An emerging international labour market?

Although international labour mobility has grown at a much slower rate than international capital mobility, there are signs that a new global labour market is emerging in which all forms of migration are growing and global supply chains are moving jobs around the world. For managerial and professional workers, the enhanced opportunity for international mobility is unquestionably advantageous. Many are moving around with secure employment contracts with national corporations or multinational ones. Others move from contract to contract, with high incomes and access to private benefits and investments. However, for a large number of others with fewer skills, many forms of insecurity and deprivation are associated with their labour mobility.

According to official data, international migrants still represent only a small proportion — about 3 per cent — of the world's population. Nevertheless, by 2000, international migrants had accounted for more than 10 per cent of the population in 70 countries, compared with 48 countries in 1970 (Global Commission on International Migration, 2005). The official figures probably understate the full extent of movement, in part because they rarely pick up clandestine movement or short-term labour circulation.

What is perhaps most interesting is that, in spite of the social disruption associated with resentment directed at migrant communities that occurs from time to time, Governments' resistance to migration seems to be declining. According to the United Nations (2006a) the proportion of Governments stating that they wished to reduce migration dropped from 40 to 22 per cent between 1996 and 2005. Many Governments have taken measures to facilitate the in migration of the types of worker they need, while 30 countries have policies to promote the inflow of highly skilled workers.

Many countries are trying to augment their supply of skilled labour by luring emigrants back home. In 2005, 72 countries had policies to encourage the return of their nationals; of those, 59 were developing countries. Meanwhile, receiving countries are increasingly adopting policies that focus on the integration of migrants. In 2005, 75 countries had programmes for integrating non-nationals, up from 52 countries in 1996.

In sum, international labour migration is already very substantial, and, while the pace of recorded migration may have slowed, a rising proportion of the world's workforce consists of migrants, with millions in clandestine situations. Although net immigration may be concentrated in a relatively small number of countries, most countries are experiencing both immigration and emigration, as well as a great deal of labour circulation.

Impact of international migration

According to ILO (2006a), there is a "global consensus" that international labour migration has a beneficial effect on growth and development in both source and destination countries. It may contribute to home-country economic development through worker remittances, the transfer of capital and skills through returning migration, and the transfer of skills and technology and investments by diasporas. It helps destination countries by filling gaps in the labour market, providing essential skills and injecting social, cultural and intellectual dynamism.

The World Bank (2005b) also claimed that an increase in migrants that would raise the workforce in high-income countries by 3 per cent by 2025 could increase global real income by 0.6 per cent, or $356 billion. Such an increase in migrant stock would be in line with the migration trend observed during the past three decades. The Bank said the relative gains would be much higher for developing-country households than for developed-country households, rivaling potential gains from global reform of merchandise trade, and estimated that $162 billion to new migrants, $143 billion to people living in developing countries (mainly by way of remittances) and $51 billion to people living in high-income countries.

However, such arguments for the beneficial effects of international migration in global aggregate terms have to be balanced by an examination of national circumstances. For instance, for developing countries, the most worrisome form of migration is that associated with the movement of the highly educated — the proverbial brain drain — although the causes may have positive aspects and the personal consequences may be beneficial, as noted earlier. A common claim is that this results in developing countries' being deprived of vitally needed skills, which deprivation impedes growth and development.

Broadly speaking, the brain drain is likely to have a much more severe effect on small countries than on large ones. While the absolute numbers working abroad may be large, some large developing countries have only about 3-5 per cent of graduates living abroad. In sub-Saharan Africa, where skilled workers make up only 4 per cent of the total workforce, they account for more than 40 per cent of those leaving the region (Özden and Schiff, 2005). Indeed, the loss of crucial skills in source countries, particularly small ones, is a cause for concern. Developing countries lose from 10 to 30 per cent of skilled workers and professionals through brain drain (International Labour Office, 2006a). Nearly 6 in every 10 highly educated migrants living in countries members of the Organization for Economic Cooperation and Development (OECD) in 2000 had originated in developing countries (United Nations, 2006b). Least developed countries are especially affected: it is estimated that about one third of migrants from Least Developed Countries to OECD countries are skilled workers (United Nations Office of the High Representative for the Least Developed countries, Landlocked Developing Countries and Small Island Developing States, and Office of the Special Adviser on Africa, 2006).

Migration, in its various forms, is an integral part of the emerging global labour market, and this movement is bound to have numerous effects on national and subnational labour markets and the character of employment and livelihoods. All forms of migration have implications for both receiving and sending societies and labour markets. While it is understandable that much of the focus should be on the migrants themselves, the fact remains that the externalities of the various forms of migration should be given more attention than has been the case.

Findings on the effect of the growing international migration on unemployment in sending and receiving labour markets are rather inconclusive. The standard theoretical position is that emigration should lower unemployment in sending areas, since the labour supply is cut; but some commentators believe that emigration is selective for the relatively employable and, by removing scarce skills, raises so-called structural unemployment.

A recent United Nations report on migration (United Nations, 2006b) stated that, although immigration may have a small adverse effect on the wages of non-migrants in receiving countries, or may raise unemployment when wages are rigid, such labour-market effects are small at the national level. It concluded that over the medium and long term, migration can generate employment and produce net fiscal gains.

ILO (2006a) has claimed that "global labour mobility ensures efficient and optimal utilization of labour," but has suggested that barriers to mobility are preventing this outcome, leading instead to more smuggling and trafficking of migrants. Other studies have suggested that countries where migrants are welcome have fewer people out of work (cited in *Financial Times*, 2006). There may, however, be no causal relationship; or migration may simply be more welcome destinations where unemployment is low.

The relation between migration and the unemployment of migrants has similarly been subject of controversy. Although some observers have questioned the widely held view that migrants have higher unemployment rates than natives, in most OECD countries with a few exceptions, the unemployment rate of young workers (aged 15-24) born abroad is higher than that of their native-born counterparts (Organization for Economic Cooperation and Development, 2006). Unemployment rates of foreign-born women (aged 15-64) are higher than that of their native-born counterparts in every OECD country without exception (Dumont and Liebig, 2005).

Migration and remittances

Migration generates a huge flow of remittances, which have become an important feature of globalization, with various effects on labour markets around the world. It is estimated that migrant workers send home remittances officially recorded at $232 billion in 2005, more than double what it had been a decade earlier. The share of global remittances going to developing countries has also increased, from 57 per cent in 1995 ($58 billion) to 72 per cent in 2005 ($167 billion) (World Bank, 2005b). This was twice the level of development aid from all sources ($100 billion a year) and was second only to FDI ($625 billion).[1] Although they may have declined owing to stricter controls since September 2001, unrecorded remittances sent through informal channels could add at least 50 per cent to the official estimates, making remittances the largest source of external capital in many developing countries.

The recent surge of officially recorded remittances partly reflects growth in the number of migrants and their incomes, but also better data reporting, diversion of remittances from informal to formal channels, and lower transfer costs and expansion of the network of remittance service providers. Nevertheless, 13 Least Developed Countries (and perhaps others) do not report remittance data and most remittances to Least Developed Countries go through informal channels (United Nations Office of the High Representative for the Least Developed countries, Landlocked Developing Countries and Small Island Developing States, and Office of the Special Adviser on Africa, 2006). Reducing transaction costs, which can be as high as 20 per cent, would promote more flows through formal channels and could increase access to financial services, including micro-credit for the poor.

The standard interpretation is that remittances result in a transfer from richer migrant-receiving countries to poorer migrant-sending countries. While this is probably correct, one should be cautious about the extent of the transfer because the flows of funds (and goods) that go with and to migrants from developing countries, both when they leave and for some time afterwards, are measured much less than remittances. Moreover, extensive research over the years has shown that remittances can be a strong force for greater social and income differentiation in the areas to which remittance income flows.

While remittances may lead to an economic transformation in rural areas, at the same time they enrich only those who receive them and may lead to land dispossession and more landlessness among those who do not benefit from such flows. This effect must be measured against the expectation that remittances can reduce rural poverty (Adams and Page, 2005).

Some household surveys suggest that remittances have been associated with significant declines in poverty (headcount) in several low-income countries (World Bank, 2005b). In addition, remittances appear to help households maintain their consumption through economic shocks and adversity. They are also associated with increased household investments in education and health, as well as increased entrepreneurship, but not with productive investments.

Remittances tend to be relatively stable financial flows, countering economic downturns in recipient countries due to financial crisis, natural disaster or civil conflict. At the macrolevel, remittances can generate foreign exchange earnings and improve the creditworthiness of a country for external borrowing. At the same time, large and sustained remittance flows can lead to currency appreciation, lower export competitiveness and dampen growth. Ghosh

(2006) warns against excessive reliance on remittances to generate growth and development as it may make recipient countries vulnerable to sudden changes in respect of remittance receipts which can be brought about by external shocks, economic mismanagement or political instability in the host countries. Ghosh cautions especially against reliance on remittances for investment-oriented purposes. Investment-oriented remittances tend to be pro-cyclical, being sensitive to changes in the business environment and highly volatile depending on the macroeconomic situation, unlike remittances used to supplement the family budget, which are generally seen as having a counter-cyclical effect, since they tend to rise in times of economic decline, helping to smooth consumption and alleviate hardship. Moreover, remittances should not be treated as a substitute for official development assistance (ODA), especially for Least Developed Countries.

At the microlevel, remittances are mainly used for consumption by recipients, addressing their basic needs in the areas of food, clothing, housing, transport, healthcare and education. There may be secondary beneficiaries in the community who gain through their employment or their purchase of locally produced goods and services. When saved, remittances may serve as safety nets for the poor. Saving and investment of remittances also increase credit availability. To the extent that they finance health and education, create employment and provide access to credit for small entrepreneurs, remittances can boost growth; to the extent that they are used for consumption, remittances can increase income levels and reduce poverty.

The perceived drawbacks of remittances (Global Commission on International Migration 2005) include the following:

- The longer migrants are abroad, the less they remit to their country of origin. Second-generation migrants are less likely to remit to the extent their parents did.

- In some countries that have sizeable numbers of citizens working abroad, large-scale remittances may be a disincentive to reforms that would provide a better basis for long-term growth.

- The benefits of remittances are not shared equally and may exacerbate the socio-economic disparities that exist between households, communities and regions in the countries of origin.

- Remittances can create a "culture of migration", encouraging young people to place excessive hopes on moving abroad.

- For some, remittances may be a disincentive to work at all.

In addition, high social costs can be incurred when migrants leave their families and communities to work abroad. The Global Commission on International Migration (2005) concluded that the pressure to remit can impose financial and psychological burdens on migrants. The World Bank (2005b), cautions against providing incentives in an attempt to direct remittances to specific areas or sectors through matching fund programmes, arguing that these schemes have had little success and that remittances should be treated like any other private income.

Box II.1
Impact of remittances in Mexico

With between 400,000 and 500,000 people leaving Mexico for the United States of America each year and an estimated 12 million Mexicans living and working illegally in the United States, the country is the biggest recipient of workers' remittances in the northern hemisphere (Lapper and Thomson, 2006). Total remittance income is expected to have approached $25 billion in 2006, having grown from only $6 billion in 2000, and is the third biggest source of foreign exchange after manufacturing and oil. Most of the money received by families in Mexico goes to consumption, but up to 20 per cent of remittances are being invested in education, housing and similar activities.

Mexican hometown associations formed by migrants living in the United States are active. There are currently over 600 Mexican hometown associations in 30 United States cities. They support public works in their localities of origin, including through funding the construction of public infrastructure, donating equipment and promoting education (Global Commission on International Migration, 2005). Schemes that allow Mexico's federal, State and municipal governments to match voluntary contributions with official funding to support road-building and other infrastructural improvements have been established for more than a decade.

Economic stability and the sheer volume of remittances, combined with the decline in average family size, have led to an impressive growth in the middle class. On one estimate, the number of families with an income of 9,000-20,000 pesos a month has doubled to 10 million in the past decade (Lapper and Thomson: 2006): but as many as 12 million Mexicans — more than one quarter of the workforce — work in the undercapitalized informal economy. Despite the success of social programmes such as Oportunidades, 8.6 million families still live in poverty. Moreover, some observers have attributed the continuing depopulation of Mexican villages to financial remittances (Lapper, 2006).

Concluding remarks

Globalization is transforming all labour-market systems and is doing so in ways that are yet to be fully understood or taken fully into account by Governments, employers and unions and others professing to represent the interests of groups of workers. Labour markets evolve all the time; but the evidence indicates that in the current phase of globalization, they have been evolving in the direction of greater levels of economic insecurity and greater levels of most forms of inequality, many of which have a direct adverse effect on the opportunity of people to live a life of decent work and satisfactory employment.

Increasingly, countries are being driven by the perceived imperative of competitiveness. International institutions, politicians and policymakers everywhere emphasize the need for national economies, enterprises and workers to become more competitive. From a social point of view, there must be limits to all this. But what should those limits be?

Another powerful lesson to have been drawn so far is the following: a precondition for liberalization's having beneficial effects for ordinary citizens is the establishment of institutions, legislation and regulations that can prevent its adverse effects from overwhelming them. This represents a different form of "conditionality" than that applied as part of the financial assistance given by the international financial Institutions in the past two decades.

Notes

[1] Ghosh (2006) points out that World Bank figures for developing countries as a group are gross flows. Deducting South-South flows and reverse flows from South to North, developing countries' net remittance receipts for 2004 amounted to just over $100 billion, against gross receipts of $160 billion.

Chapter III

Social groups in the labour force

The advance of globalization has had important implications for work and employment outcomes in all countries. However, changes in international and national markets for labour have presented different sets of challenges for different groups in society. Some of these social groups are more visible than others and have managed to dominate the debate on work and labour. The lack of visibility of other groups requires vigorous and sustained action to ensure that their particular concerns and challenges are recognized and adequately addressed by policymakers.

The transformation of work and employment can be seen in the changing patterns of the family, of generational groups in the family, and of society at large. These changes translate into the fact that different types of work and employment are being sought by different groups, including children, young people, women and older persons, which have different relationships with the realities of work and labour. Particularly for the first three groups, issues related to education and poverty drive and shape their perspectives of the labour market and their participation in it. Poverty and education will thus be common threads throughout this chapter.

It is also important to understand and address the challenges in respect of a second cluster of social groups. While the needs of each group are distinct from the needs of the others, these groups — persons with disabilities, indigenous peoples and migrants — are clearly vulnerable and in dire need of greater policy attention. Although these groups are extremely diverse in the geographical, economic, social and political sense, they all share a common expectation of full and productive participation in the labour market.

Work in a changing family context

Work has traditionally been based on a family division of labour. In every society, rich or poor, each member of a typical family relies on the work contribution of others. The family structure moulds the work pattern, and patterns of work and labour in the economy shape the family.

The family has undergone a significant transformation in all parts of the world, one largely determined by economic development and demographic transition. With globalization, it is becoming increasingly fragile and diverse. Demographic changes have changed the types, characteristics and age structure of the membership of the family. The extended family, which used to be the traditional family model in developing countries and the main support network, is gradually disappearing. At the same time, the nuclear family continues to be the predominant model in developed countries, although its structure no longer represents that of the majority of families.

In addition, there is an increasing globalization phenomenon of household labour "chains", that is to say, the pattern of temporary or long-term migration of household members. As the international labour system takes shape in the twenty-first century, one can anticipate that the dispersed family will take on an increasingly international form, with certain family members temporarily migrating abroad for long periods, and believing they will rejoin their family while in some cases actually never doing so.

The changing family structure as well as increasing numbers of older persons and the erosion of familial support systems has serious implications for the care and well-being of older persons. Most of the burden of caring for older family members falls on women. In some regions, the family remains the most important source of support for the elderly, although there are changes that are undermining this traditional means of support. Increases in population at older ages and in their need for services put the burden on social protection systems and challenge the ability of public, private and community institutions to respond with commitment to equity among social groups. Many countries cannot afford the costly investments in institutional care.

These changes in the family include the continuing feminization of labour, characterized by the fact that many more jobs are being taken by women, by growing precariousness, by a convergence in levels of female labour-force participation with those of men, and by changes in the concept of wages, including the demise of the family wage.

Working patterns are influenced by the changing patterns of marriage, fertility, morbidity and mortality. Fertility has been decreasing in most regions as a result of urbanization, rising level of education, increased age at marriage and the more widespread practice of family planning. Clearly, different parts of the world are at different stages of demographic transition; on the other hand, the share of the world's population in the older age brackets has been rising very considerably.

In Africa, high fertility rates have led to an increase in the number of potential workers. The working-age population increased from about 281 million in 1985 to 375 million in 1995 and to 489 million in 2005. According to the United Nations, by 2015, the working-age population is projected to reach 616 million people, implying a sharp increase in the supply of labour, which will need to be met by an equivalent increase in income-earning opportunities. Several socioeconomic and cultural factors have contributed to the persistently high fertility rates in Africa, including low levels of education for girls and lack of job opportunities for women, inadequate access to contraceptives, and poor access to health care and education, which hamper skill development and limit employment opportunities. At the same time, HIV/AIDS and the resurgence of malaria and tuberculosis have had an adverse impact on life expectancy and the capabilities of the working-age population.

Africa has been hit hardest by the HIV/AIDS pandemic, as all the countries with an adult prevalence rate of 20 per cent or more are in Southern Africa (Joint United Nations Programme on HIVAIDS (UNAIDS), 2004). In this context, not only are a few countries experiencing a negative population growth rate, but some countries have something close to a U-shaped age distribution of their population, with large numbers of children and very large numbers of orphans, alongside a fairly large number of older persons.

This has affected the makeup of family membership and shaped patterns of work and labour, leading to pressure on children and teenagers to find income-earning activity, as well as on many older people to continue to work into old age, both because they lack the income from children who have died in their prime and because they have the added responsibility of looking after orphans. It is believed that there is an ongoing loss of intergenerational transfer of skills and knowledge and household and community solidarity which will make it difficult to implement any conventional employment strategy.

By contrast, in some Western European countries and Japan, where the fertility rates have fallen below the population reproduction rate, two demographic developments have emerged, namely an expanding ageing process and a shrinking population. This has caused concern in some countries, leading to the introduction of pro-natalist policies, including longer maternity leave and financial assistance for childcare. So far, such policies seem to have had little effect, although they have tended to benefit couples who have children relative to those who do not.

The sustained drop in fertility in Latin America presents challenges, among them, creation of jobs for a growing female labour supply compatible with chil-drearing and educational options for young people (Economic Commission for Latin America and the Caribbean, 2004). In many countries in Asia, the partici-pation of women in the labour force is constrained by factors such as the lack of flexibility in career and child-rearing, the lack of day-care facilities for children, and the lack of home care for older persons (Economic and Social Commission for Asia and the Pacific, 2005). Policies designed to help meet the demands of family life, as well as policies that provide support for the care of children and older persons, are needed.

Women: greater participation, greater risks

Since the Fourth World Conference on Women held in 1995, important progress in the promotion of women's economic rights and independence has been made, although deep inequalities remain (United Nations, 2004d) Women represent an increasing share of the world's labour force — ranging from at least a third of the labour force in most countries to close to half in some countries in Europe (International Labour Organization, 2006a).

The share of women in wage employment in the non-agricultural sector, which is one of the four indicators under Millennium Development Goal 3, is intended to measure the degree to which labour markets are open to women in the industry and services sector. However, to achieve gender equality in the labour market, other factors have to be addressed, including occupational segre-gation, gender wage gaps, women's disproportionate representation in informal employment and unpaid work and higher unemployment rates.[1] In the present section, we will review four issues that affect the status of women in the world of work: (a) women's participation in the labour force, (b) women's participation in the informal sector, (c) occupational segregation and (d) reconciliation of work and family responsibilities.

Women's participation in the labour force

Female labour-force participation rates — the proportion of women recorded as being in the labour force, either working for income or seeking employment —

have risen in most countries of the world, partly as a result of increased access for women to education and to participation in political decision-making. A wide range of gender-sensitive policies and programmes at the country level have focused on creating an enabling environment for women's participation in paid work and self-employment. However, in Eastern Europe, the transition to a market economy in the early 1990s led to some decline in women's share in the labour force from previously high levels (International Labour Organization, 2006a).

Women's participation in the informal sector

Although female employment has increased, this has been paralleled in some countries by a deterioration in the terms and conditions of employment in many areas. The growth of informal work across the world, along with the informalization or casualization of formal employment, has allowed employers to lower labour costs. Women tend to be overrepresented in the informal sector and in self-employment where jobs are lower-paying and less secure. At the same time, they are less likely than men to be covered by social security schemes, another hidden cost of precarious employment.

In many countries, women are disproportionately represented in casual jobs (Campbell and Brosnan, 2005; Fuller and Vosko, 2005; Gootfried, Nishiwara, and Aiba, K, 2006). Women who have casual jobs are often excluded from labour statistics and often overlooked by labour inspection systems. Contractualization is another related global trend that affects women disproportionately and, in this regard, there must be concern that women will have less satisfactory contracts because of their weaker bargaining position and widespread preconceptions about women's degree of attachment to pursuing a labour career.

Occupational segregation

Horizontal segregation and vertical segregation are detrimental to women's participation in the labour market. While horizontal segregation prevents women from entering traditional 'male occupations', vertical segregation impacts on women's career development opportunities preventing them from reaching managerial positions.

Women's opportunities to participate in the labour force have expanded in recent decades; however, the fact remains that the occupations traditionally engaged in by women pay less than jobs requiring similar skill levels but held predominately by men. In virtually all countries, women are overrepresented in the service sector and men are overrepresented in the industrial sector (Anker, 2006).

Gender segregation by occupation reinforces gender stereotypes in society and a labour-market rigidity that reduces efficiency and growth. According to the International Labour Organization (ILO): "Women continue to face discrimination in recruitment for employment and barriers to occupational mobility. Different values and remuneration continue to be attached to men's and women's jobs, so that labour markets are still characterized by wage differentials and discrimination on the basis of sex."[2]

Gender wage gaps persist in all sectors and throughout the world, largely owing to occupational segregation, both vertical and horizontal, and as a result of women's high rate of participation in part-time work. Studies of the more rapidly growing Asian economies suggest that the growth in exports of labour-intensive manufactured goods and economic growth have been most rapid in those countries that had the widest gender wage gaps. The downward pressure on wages in the jobs concerned, which is a result of global competition, places serious limits on women's bargaining power and wages. Accordingly, it is structurally difficult to raise women's wages and close the gender wage gap.

Reconciliation of work and family responsibilities

There are significant cross-national differences in the rate of female labour-force participation. Since women are considered responsible for caring of children and the elderly, they often face difficulties in balancing work and family responsibilities. Countries have taken steps to make available child and elderly care to relieve women of this burden. Policies aimed at women (rather than at parents or caregivers), however, can reinforce the perception that women are responsible for household work.

Evidence suggests that where childcare is readily available and compatible with work schedules, more women work outside the home (van der Lippe and van Dijk, 2002). Where policies support maternity and paternity leave, are flexible for women returning to work after childbearing, and include the availability of part-time work, more women work outside the home. The increasing use of information and communication technologies (ICT) has also created new forms of employment that allow women and men to telework or work from home.

Countries are also increasingly encouraging men to support women by sharing the unpaid work in the family (United Nations, 2004d).

The increase in the number of women working outside the home poses a dilemma for social integration. Often, work outside the home is accompanied by less time spent in traditional roles such as caring for children and preparing meals. Frequently, conflicting pressures, associated with the desire to fulfil domestic roles and pursue work outside the home, result in an internal struggle for many women faced with a trade-off between home and professional life. Men face similar challenges. Both roles are important for different aspects of social integration. On one level, socialization of children and family maintenance are activities essential to ensuring that children and families are integrated. Parental support helps to ensure that children stay in school and complete their homework. Preparing meals is an essential activity supportive of health and nutrition, which allow children and employed family members to engage in their role as student or worker. Often, working parents, especially women, find the two roles rewarding and valuable, but are left with too few hours in the day to fulfil both, especially if circumstances require working long hours or multiple jobs. As more women throughout the world work outside the home, they often continue to do traditional work inside it, creating a "double shift", that is to say, a situation where they work full-time outside the home, then come home and provide essentially full-time care for the family as well. Social policies and measures to facilitate the reconciliation of work and family responsibilities for both women and men should be the focus of policymakers if they intend to support women's empowerment through participation in the workplace.

In conclusion, during recent decades, labour markets have become increasingly feminized, yet women's employment in many sectors continues to be highly volatile, much more so than men's. As we have seen, the great disadvantage for women, compared with the men, is that they must balance labour-market work with domestic work. A strategy, extending beyond the fostering of greater participation by women, is also needed to address the several layers of discrimination, including horizontal and vertical occupational segregation, in an integrated manner. All policies should be mindful of the need to support both women and men in their multiple roles and to destroy stereotypes of gender roles in order to promote the empowerment of women through equal participation in the labour force.

Ending child labour

Today, as in the past, most children are growing up in a caring family environment, enjoying family bonding, proper health care and nutrition, and enrolment in basic education. Yet, there are still too many for whom this healthy and nourishing environment is not a given. Some 190 million children under age 14 are now engaged in some form of work.

Defining "child labour" is not a straightforward task. Work done by children ranges from domestic and unpaid family work to wage work (both for cash and for in-kind payments) and differs in terms of hours (full-time versus part-time) and intensity (light versus heavy). In view of the negative connotation of the term "child labour", a distinction is often made between harmful "child labour" and the much broader category of (potentially beneficial) child work. However, considering the diversity of children's work, this dichotomy seems simplistic. The establishment of continuum proceeding from the most hazardous to the most beneficial forms of child labour may constitute a more useful approach (Boyden, Ling and Myers, 1998).

Estimates of child labour

The incidence of child labour varies considerably across regions, sectors and age groups. Almost two thirds of working children live in Asia and the Pacific. However, the proportion is highest in sub-Saharan Africa, where more than 25 per cent of children work (International Labour Organization, 2006b, para. 30). Child labour is more prevalent in rural than in urban areas. The vast majority of working children are engaged in agricultural work or work in the informal sector, and less than 5 per cent work in export industries. Everywhere, older children and adolescents are more likely to work than younger children, and the majority of children do not work full-time (Boyden, Ling and Myers, 1998).

The participation rates of boys and girls in economic activities are roughly equal (International Labour Organization, 2002b; International Labour Organization, 2006b). However, girls usually have fewer work options than boys and thus fewer possibilities to escape oppressive work situations (Boyden, Ling and Myers, 1998). Boys typically participate more in wage work and in household enterprises; girls tend to be involved in domestic activities (Grootaert and Kanbur, 1995; Ilahi, 2001). Girls begin working at an earlier age, particularly in rural areas. Their outside work is often of low status, and they frequently earn less than boys and have less control over their earnings. Combining outside work with domestic chores and school imposes a triple burden on girls, affecting their school attendance and performance. Although girls seem to be more concerned about the dangerous conditions of their work, it is boys who are more often engaged in hazardous activities, particularly with increasing age (Haspels, Romeijn and Schroth, 2000; Swaminathan, 1998; Woodhead, 1998; International Labour Organization, 2002b; 2006b).

Recent ILO estimates (2006b, table I.1) point to a rapid reduction in child labour, in particular of its worst forms: the total number of child labourers aged 5-17 fell by 11 per cent worldwide (from 245 million to 218 million) in the period 2000 - 2004. It is noteworthy that the largest decrease is occurring in the area of hazardous work. In general, the more harmful the work and the more vulnerable the children involved, the faster has been the decline in child labour in recent years. The incidence of hazardous child labour declined by 26 per cent (from 170 million to 126 million) for children aged 5-17 and by 33 per cent (from 111 million to 74 million) among those aged 5-14. In light of the encouraging global trend, ILO (ibid., para. 33) claims that the elimination of the worst forms of child labour in the next 10 years is feasible.[3]

Stark regional differences prevail in terms of progress. The decline has largely been driven by a rapid decrease in child labour in Latin America and the Caribbean, where the number of economically active children decreased by two thirds, leaving only 5 per cent of children engaged in work, according to ILO estimates. In sub-Saharan Africa, by contrast, the absolute number of working children actually increased, partly owing to high rates of population growth and the economic hardships resulting from the spread of HIV/AIDS.

Determinants of child labour

The root causes of child labour are complex. They can be divided into factors affecting labour supply and those affecting labour demand. One of the main determinants of children's labour supply is poverty.[4] At the national level, a negative relationship exists between a country's income per capita and children's labour-force participation. This relationship is strongest for the least developed countries and becomes less marked for middle-income countries. The structure of production — and thus the level of economic development — also plays a role, with shares of agriculture in gross domestic product (GDP) being positively correlated with the incidence of child labour (Fallon and Tzannatos, 1998).[5] At the household level, low income is the single most important predictor of child labour (Dehejia and Gatti, 2002). Working children's contributions typically account for 10-30 per cent of total household income (Bhalotra, 2000)[6]. Since poor families spend, on average, 80 per cent of their income on food, these contributions to family income are often essential for survival (Anker, 2000).

A low health and education status, vulnerability and voicelessness are additional dimensions of poverty contributing to child labour. First, illness (such as HIV/AIDS) or death of household members can draw children into wage work in order that they may provide a substitute for lost income and can raise the domestic workload of girls in particular (Moore, 2000; Ilahi, 2001). Second, children may be driven to work by the inaccessibility of schools, the low quality of education (which makes it rational to work), the cost of schooling, or violence and humiliation experienced from teachers and classmates (Woodhead, 1998). Third, vulnerability is a key determinant of child labour. Children's employment is frequently a livelihood strategy which serves to minimize the risk of income losses, for example, through adult unemployment or crop failure. Children affected by crises such as economic shocks, natural disasters or conflict are also at high risk of being required to begin to work. A final dimension of poverty contributing to child labour is voicelessness and powerlessness. Poor workers typically must accept the wages that they are offered, even if, these are insufficient to support a family, thereby making child labour necessary for family survival. Moreover, they may not be able to organize into trade unions or other types of workers' organizations, which have been crucial in effecting a reduction in child labour (Fyfe and Jankanish, 1997; Tabusa, 2000).

Child labour is not only a consequence but also a cause of poverty. A vicious circle of poverty can be created when poor parents send their children to work, thereby jeopardizing school attendance and performance and thus their children's future earnings. Child labour may also exacerbate the youth employment problem if it prevents children from obtaining education and skills required to compete on the labour market as young adults.[7]

Poverty, although a decisive factor, is insufficient to explain the existence of the child labour supply: the poorest regions are not always those with the highest incidence of child labour. Other factors include social norms, household size and mother's labour-force participation, imperfect credit markets and economic incentives. Finally, it is important not to disregard children's own motivations. Children's responses to studies that attempted to capture children's perspectives of their working lives show that they often perceive work as a natural and necessary aspect of childhood and as part of their identity. Most children work only part-time. Their income helps them make an economic contribution to their family and gives them recognition, self-esteem and increased bargaining power. Children also value the friendships and fun experienced during work (Woodhead, 1998). While experience, in terms of years worked, does not seem to raise future earnings (Grimsrud, 2003; Swaminathan, 1998), work can teach children skills that are of importance in their future lives.

Although less researched than the determinants of labour supply, the factors affecting labour demand are also important. The main factors influencing demand for child labour are the belief that children are more docile or better able to perform certain tasks than adults (the "nimble fingers" argument), the relative importance of the informal versus the formal sector, and the prevailing production technology (Grootaert and Kanbur, 1995). Low wages paid to children also influence the demand for their labour.

Action against child labour

Policy choices crucially affect some of the determinants of child labour described above. Lack of political commitment on the part of the government has repeatedly been identified as one of the main obstacles to reducing child labour (see, for example, Boyden and Myers, 1995). In recent years, however, political consensus on the need to eliminate child labour has increased. This is illustrated by the rapidly growing number of ratifications of international instruments calling for an end to child labour such as International Labour Conventions, No. 138; concerning Minimum Age for Admission to Employment; and No. 182, concerning the Prohibition and Immediate Action for the Elimination of the Worst Forms of Child Labour. The issue of child labour also received significant attention at the 2002 twenty-seventh special session of the United Nations General Assembly on children and was mentioned in the 2005 World Summit Outcome.[8] Despite the strong political commitment at the international level to eliminating the worst forms of child labour, effective mobilization within relevant ministries, departments and agencies at national and local levels has yet to occur in many countries (International Labour Organization, 2006b).

Owing to the multiple determinants of child labour, any strategy to eliminate child labour must address a wide range of causes. A comprehensive approach combining complementary actions on the legal, educational, economic and cultural fronts is needed.

In addition to efforts to reduce poverty, two government interventions frequently used in the fight against child labour include minimum age legislation and compulsory education. A ban on child labour acts as a deterrent and a basis for preventive and punitive measures (Jankanish, 2000). Legislation can have a lasting effect on perceptions: by changing what people are used to, bans affect what is considered "natural" and moral. However, they are difficult to enforce and could harm the welfare of poor households relying on child labour as part of a livelihood strategy. By driving the problem underground, regulation may hinder the provision of support and protection to working children (Woodhead, 1998).

Minimum age legislation and compulsory education can be mutually reinforcing. By making education an obligation, rather than a right, legislation can significantly contribute to changing parents' attitudes towards child labour (Boyden and Myers, 1995). Nevertheless, it is frequently not enforced, particularly in rural areas which often lack schools; and if family survival depends on children's earnings, compulsory education may result in an excessive workload for children who have to combine school and work. Flexible arrangements that will allow working children to continue education would be more constructive, and should be implemented to supplement compulsory education.

In addition to adopting legislative approaches, national Governments can contribute to reducing child labour through public expenditures on social services. By improving children's survival chances, expenditures on health and sanitation may reduce fertility and thus the potential supply of child workers (Cigno, Rosati and Guarcello, 2002). Expenditures on education are crucial in that quality education not only increases the alternatives available to children (both now and in the future), but also raises children's awareness of their rights and of the dangers of work.

To reduce the direct and indirect costs associated with education, some countries have developed innovative incentives for schooling, such as cash transfers dependent on children's school attendance, scholarships, food-for-school programmes[9] and the provision to schoolchildren of school supplies, uniforms, meals and essential health services. Other incentives include improved school quality (including curricula, accessibility and staffing), childcare facilities and separate toilets for girls so as to facilitate girls' attendance. The measure of offering practical skills and vocational training at school may be a means to increase the relevance of education and to ensure parents' support.

In addition to reducing the costs, Governments can stimulate children's school attendance by making it easier to combine work and school, for example, by offering a choice between day and evening classes.[10] Such approaches are problematic, however, if they excessively reduce the total number of hours spent at school. Since child workers may be too old or may have trouble adapting to the routine of school life, non-formal education is crucial to facilitating working children's entry into the normal school system and may be the only form of education available to older children (Haspels, de los Angeles-Bautista and Rialp, 2000).

Policies focusing on poverty reduction, legislation and universal education should be complemented by policies to encourage changes in technology and improve the adult labour market (International Labour Organization, 2006b). The protection of workers' rights is an important component of comprehensive approaches to tackling child labour. Although a narrow focus on child labour helps obtain commitment from a range of actors, a wider approach focusing on general labour standards (in particular adult wage rates) may have a larger impact and ultimately reach more children.

A crucial component of interventions to eliminate child labour is access to far-reaching social programmes that help turn around the vicious circle of poverty. In addition to free and quality education (including non-formal education), these should include safety nets, access to health services, pre-vocational and technical training, in-kind assistance to children removed from work, and income-generating measures for family members (including credit and savings programmes). Since perceptions of child labour as "natural" perpetuate its existence, measures to tackle it must also address societal preconceptions through awareness-raising among children, parents, teachers, employers, religious figures and community leaders.

For interventions to be effective, they must be well-sequenced and time frames must be of sufficient length. In particular, programmes monitoring the removal of child labour from certain industries should not begin before social protection components have been introduced and become effective (as was the case in some past interventions to eliminate child labour).

Considering the economic reality faced by working children and their families, short- and long-term goals of interventions must differ. In the short run, children involved in the hazardous and worst forms of child labour need to be the focus of removal and rehabilitation measures, whereas children engaged in non-harmful work will benefit most from interventions designed to improve their work situation. In the long run, interventions must provide households with viable alternatives to child labour.

Youth: unemployment, inactivity and education

Young people constitute about one fifth of the world's population, and half of the total unemployed global workforce. It is estimated that those aged 15-24 accounted for some 89 million of the total 192 million people out of work in 2005 (International Labour Organization, 2006c). Youth are the first generation to feel the full effects of globalization on their choices in respect of education, training and work and, indeed, on their full transition into society.

Some 1.1 billion people worldwide are young people. The vast majority of them, some 85 per cent, live in developing countries (United Nations, 2006c). Tremendous progress has been achieved in improving the well-being of the current generation of youth compared with previous ones. Owing to better maternal and child health care and improvements in nutrition, child survival rates in developing countries have steadily increased over the past decades and have contributed to the presence of an ever-larger number of young people in developing countries. The demographic growth of the youth cohort in those countries has been partly offset by stabilizing or declining fertility in many developed countries. Still, the number of youth had almost doubled from 560 million in 1965 to 1,020 million in 1995. In the past 10 years, 133 million people were added which today comprises to a total of 1,158 million young people.

Youth in the globalized world of work

The general environment in which young people are making their transition into society at the beginning of the twenty-first century is characterized by a number of features, some emerging and some persisting. The latter category includes poverty and education; the former, globalization and migration as well as the use of media and technology.

Many of the world's youth live in poverty. It is estimated that one fifth of the total global youth population (over 200 million) live on less than $1 per day and that roughly one in every two young men and women (515 million) live on below $2 per day (United Nations, 2004c). The plight of the working poor among young people is an issue that has only recently started to gain attention (International Labour Organization, 2006c).

Many young people apply individual strategies to cope with poverty. The informal sector is where most seek income, often through self-employment or through informal networks of peers or elders, and increasingly in large urban settings with little support from the family networks existing in rural areas. Another approach to addressing poverty, namely, entry or re-entry into the education system, is often not an option. Indeed, the stereotypic connotation of "youth unemployment" — as referring to youth that are leisurely seeking jobs after having completed their formal education — does not apply to these groups: young people living in poverty can generally not afford to be unemployed.

There have been very notable achievements in the area of education over the past decades and new generations have, logically, benefited most from those. More children than before are completing a full course of primary schooling; and in most regions, four out of five eligible young people are currently enrolled in some form of secondary education. In addition, the number of young people who are entering tertiary education has grown beyond the 100 million mark (United Nations Educational, Scientific and Cultural Organization, 2006). This has had substantive effects on their employment situation.

However, the educational success of the current generation of youth is incomplete. A total of 130 million young people, (roughly 1 in every 10 young persons) are illiterate, having missed out on, or been forced to drop out of, primary education during their childhood. Young women are overrepresented in this group. Also, some 100 million eligible children are currently not in school, mostly in sub-Saharan Africa and parts of South Asia (United Nations Children's Fund, 2004). It is likely that a majority of those children will, in the coming years, replace the current group of illiterate youth. Achievement of the Millennium Development Goal of universal primary education will be of direct benefit in enabling future generations of young people to be prepared for negotiating their individual transitions successfully.

Achievements in both basic and higher education for young men, and increasingly for young women, have created a larger, better-educated generation. This has directly resulted in higher expectations among young people when they enter the world of work. Unfortunately, in many cases, the economies in which they live have been unable to provide opportunities that match these expectations. The inability of those economies to absorb the large group of well-educated students has led to many instances of friction among students who feel increased pressure to stand out among a tight pack of talented achievers.

In this environment, countries that have been able to benefit from globalization have witnessed an occupational shift in employment from rural and small-scale occupations towards jobs in export-oriented manufacturing of goods and services in, or close to, urban centres. Young people, with their flexibility and mobility, have particularly benefited from this trend. The global shift of manufacturing from developed to developing countries has allowed many young people in developing countries to benefit from these job opportunities.

One could argue that young people are winners in the globalization game, particularly those able to use their competitive advantage in technology-related employment. Yet, for every manufacturing position created for a young person in a rapidly growing economy, another opportunity for a manufacturing job is oftentimes lost elsewhere. At the same time, there are many young people that have not benefited from the economic globalization process. For many young people in Africa, South Asia and Latin America, few real opportunities exist as a result of globalization and the spread of information and communication technologies. Yet, global media make young people increasingly aware of their place in society — not only of their economic status and position, but also of their own political participation — and have further contributed to their high expectations (United Nations, 2002b).

Thus poverty, educational achievement, inability to find jobs at home, and political dissatisfaction all push young people to migrate in search of opportunities. A survey of young people in the Arab world in 2004 indicated that some 75 per cent would emigrate to Europe or the United States of America if given the opportunity (United Nations Development Programme, 2005a). Yet, the international climate for young job-seekers is not too favourable. Recipient Governments are keen to cherry-pick only those with elite educational qualifications, mostly from Western universities; select only those with proved skills that are in short supply locally; or position immigrants towards short-term employment contracts with no options for extended stays. Hence, in terms of economic development and self-realization, much talent is lost when it cannot be steered towards a willing employer or a self-entrepreneurial activity.

Youth inactivity and youth unemployment

Over the past decades, youth inactivity, defined as not being in the labour force, has increased. The education sector has been able to absorb and retain more young people outside the labour force, increasingly beyond the upper age limit of youth, namely, age 24. As a result, between 1995 and 2005, while the total youth population grew by some 13 per cent, the youth labour force grew by only 5 per cent. Worldwide, the number of young people employed declined from 52 per cent of all youth in 1995 to 47 per cent 2005 (table III.1). The fact that, globally, youth unemployment is growing ant that unemployment rose from 74 million in 1995 to 89 million at present (International Labour Organization, 2006c) indicates an unsettling trend.

There is, however, a large discrepancy between regions. While there were declines in the youth labour force in both the developed countries and the countries of East Asia, the youth labour force has grown by about 30 per cent since 1995 in the Middle East and Northern African region, as well as in sub-Saharan Africa where the youth labour force grew almost as rapidly as the youth population. In regions where unemployment among the educated is high, higher education contributes to increased inactivity in two ways. First, as pointed out earlier, students attending higher educational institutions full-time are counted as economically inactive. Second, because youth economic inactivity includes young people who are neither in employment nor in education, university graduates unable to find suitable jobs are added to their ranks. Young people who are neither in employment nor in education also include "inactive non-students", namely, those who are engaged in household duties or care for other household members, live with a disability or are ill, or do not know how to look for work or believe that there is no work (discouraged workers). Some of the data available are presented in table III.1.

A main conclusion to be drawn from the table is that whereas it is important to study unemployment rates, normally indicating those youth in the labour force who are without work, it is also necessary to consider the very large group of young people outside the labour force who are also inactive (as shown in line 8 of the table). The size of this group is not known exactly, as only some regional estimates are available. From the available data, it could be estimated that in 2005 some 170 million youth were economically inactive worldwide, although this group might well have been active in the informal sector.

The policy response

Globally, the level of youth unemployment and inactivity should be a matter for serious concern. For individuals, long-term unemployment can lead to margin-

Table III.1.
Estimates of youth inactivity, 2005
(Millions)

		World	Ded/ EU	CEE	EA	SEA/P	SA	LAC	MENA	SSA
1	Total youth population	1158	124	71	230	109	289	105	83	147
2	In the labour force	633	65	30	155	62	137	57	33	96
3	Employed	548	56	24	142	52	123	48	25	79
4	Unemployed	85	9	6	12	10	14	3	9	17
5	Not in the labour force	525	60	41	75	47	153	48	50	51
6	- In education	440	52	23	..	..	..	30	..	28
7	- Not in education	85	8	18	...	...	..	19	..	22
8	NEET = lines 4 plus line 7	170	17	24	...	..	..	22	..	39
9	NEET percentage	15	13	34	..	..	..	21	..	27

Source: International Labour Organization, 2006c, tables 2.2 and 2.4; and sources quoted in figure 4.3. See ILO for details on specific countries in regions.

Note: Two dots (..) indicate that data are not available. Figures in italics are estimates made on the basis of existing data.

Abbreviations: NEET, neither in employment nor in education; Ded/Eu, developed countries and European Union; CEE , Central and Eastern Europe; EA, East Asia; SEA/P, South-eastern Asia and the Pacific; SA, South Asia; LAC, Latin America and the Caribbean; MENA, Middle East and Northern Africa; SSA, sub-Saharan Africa.

alization, frustration, low self- esteem and, sometimes, acts that burden society (United Nations, 2004a). In the long term, longitudinal data in the United States suggest that young men who had experienced long periods of unemployment suffered from lower wages in the jobs that they eventually found, experienced increased chances of repeated unemployment in the future and had a higher likelihood of longer unemployment spells in their adult careers (Mroz and Savage, 2001). Evidence from South-eastern Europe suggests that long-term unemployment also increases the risk of income poverty (Kolev and Saget, 2005). Because long-term unemployed youth will be a burden on public budgets, it is important to offer "second chances", both in education and in employment, for those unable to secure a successful transition the first time around (World Bank, 2006a).

Yet, skepticism persists about the negative effects of youth unemployment and youth inactivity on the well-being and employment outcomes of young people. Some of the arguments are generational in nature. Many policymakers (and parents) who have argued that in the previous generations, a young individual working through the educational system would eventually find a decent job opportunity, ignore the fact that current generations in their country enjoy almost universal secondary education, yet are required to compete for far fewer jobs. It is, for example, often noted that young people tend to need some time in navigating their transitions into adulthood and that a short period of unemployment is a fairly harmless and even helpful part of that transition. A related argument is that it is only those youth that can afford to be unemployed who are in fact formally unemployed.

There are other doubts expressed about the seriousness of youth unemployment. Youth unemployment is strongly correlated with the cyclic nature of the labour market in any country. As less experienced entrants into the labour market, youth have a disadvantage when compared with older workers with higher productivity during an economic downturn. While youth unemployment can thus be viewed as merely an indicator of the economy's temporary downturn, it does not diminish the negative effects of long-term inactivity experienced by young people.

In their policy responses, rather than concentrate on pro-poor economic growth or job creation, Governments tend to focus on the supply side of the labour market, addressing perceived weaknesses of youth in terms of their lack of skills or their attitudes (United Nations, 2002b). These measures perceive young people as a vulnerable group in need of support, rather than as an asset (Curtain, 2006). Yet there are other measures that can be taken whereby young people are perceived as an asset. For those living in poverty, actions should be taken to strengthen their entrepreneurial and innovative skills, and assist them by providing microcredit services for self-employment. For those with a track record in the formal education system and high expectations, domestic job creation and job placement should be encouraged, complemented by more large-scale overseas temporary work opportunities. While the cost of these interventions and their benefits are not easily measured and appreciated (World Bank, 2006a), they will help unleash some of the untapped potential of the current generation.

Implications for education, schooling and work

The centrality of education and training for young people warrants some reflections on their merits in the era of globalization. In societies where there is an overwhelming urge to make more people competitive, productive and able to obtain and retain jobs, the educational system is at risk of preparing people to become job holders without attention to the issue of greater individual fulfilment. Yet, schooling is about more than just preparing people for jobs: it is about exposing them to a broad education and culture. Expressions of the understandable desire to ensure that young people emerge equipped to engage in available income-earning activities have long been subject to the objection that too narrow a focus on that objective can result in an excessively utilitarian approach, stultifying human development rather than liberating the creativity and innovative capacities of the young. Indeed, it may well be necessary for there to be a trade-off between cultural aims of education and the need for young people to be equipped to survive and prosper amid the realities of their local and national labour markets.

Distinctions between schooling and training are becoming blurred; and training is itself in crisis to the extent that it has focused largely on the needs of formal enterprises (International Labour Organization, 2003a). The challenge here is to reposition the ideas of skill training within a context of capability development. That what today's employers want may differ considerably from what today's young citizens want is a matter for concern. Some analysts argue that national educational and training schemes should be integrated and deliberately tailored to the wishes and needs of local or multinational employers. This harks back to the old and now-discredited manpower planning models that were in vogue in the later stages of the pre-globalization era. Any such approach would be hard enough to implement efficiently and equitably in a closed economy; it would be much harder to sustain in the emerging circumstances of highly open economies where future structures of demand are so much more unpredictable. Moreover, there is a more important moral dimension. Such an approach leads to a narrow functionalism, in which broad cultural education would be reserved for elites while job-preparation courses would be left to the masses, limiting social mobility and entrenching on education-based social dualism.

Other ideas are gaining ground. One popular idea is that of lifelong learning which is attractive if seen as offering the opportunity to learn and refine one's capabilities as and when one wishes. The idea becomes less attractive if, however, what is implied is having, at the whim of others and in a state of constant insecurity, to learn new skills that become obsolescent at regular intervals of a few months. The tendency within the globalization and flexibility model is to exert pressure on behalf of the latter aspect as when policymakers who speak of human resources development focus exclusively on making people more employable. More attention could perhaps be given to ensuring employment structures that allow workers to use and develop their capabilities, thereby retooling jobs rather than just retooling workers.

Finally, what has been called community-based training has gained support in the international donor and technical assistance community, primarily as a means of boosting basic skills of workers in the informal economy in developing countries. Although such training does seem attractive, it should be carefully evaluated: insofar as it is government- or donor-led, the administrative costs may be larger than envisaged. The real question, however, for those advocating this route is whether such schemes are filling a real need or are substituting for what would be provided anyway. Subsidized schemes also raise questions regarding the appropriateness of the selection of those skills on which the community-based training schemes choose to concentrate as well as the appropriateness of the displacement of others. They could also end up helping the less vulnerable in the local community rather than the most vulnerable, reflecting a tendency for such schemes to take the best possible trainees so as to maximize success.

Training is an area of work that is easily captured by interest-based rhetoric. Employers, who obviously benefit from having a pool of workers with skills that they can utilize are inclined to claim that the government is not investing enough in training and to demand subsidies so as to provide training themselves. Those claims and demands are perfectly understandable, since they would tend to lower employers' cost and raise their net profits. However, what is preferable, or of higher priority, is a regulatory framework that would enable firms and workers, young and no longer young, to benefit from employer training schemes. This should include measures to ensure proper standards and certification, including a legitimate system of national qualifications, and institutional respect for apprenticeship schemes.

Active ageing and work

The world population is ageing rapidly, and this trend is expected to continue well into the twenty-first century. A major factor contributing to this change is the decline in fertility rates and increases in life expectancy. In the 1950s, older persons[11] represented 8 per cent of the population and in 2000, 10 per cent. Projections for the population of older persons globally in the year 2050 are expected to reach 21 per cent. By that time, the number of older persons in the world will have surpassed the youth population for the first time in history (United Nations, 2002a).

There are significant differences between the developed world and the less developed world in terms of the numbers and proportions of older persons. Rising longevity is taking place mainly in developing countries. A substantial majority of older persons — over 60 per cent — are living in developing countries, where the growth in the numbers of older persons has come at lower levels of income and lower levels of institutional capacity than in developed countries (Eberstadt, 2005). In less developed regions, 50 per cent of older males and 19 per cent of older females are economically active, as compared with 21 per cent of older males and 10 per cent of older females in developed regions. Increased wealth and urbanization in member countries of the Organization for Economic Cooperation and Development (OECD) have led to longer education, shorter working lives and longer retirement periods (Auer and Fortuny, 2000). The greater labour participation rates of older persons in developing countries are largely due to lack of financial support for older persons, making retirement a luxury difficult to attain (United Nations, 2002a). While people in less developed countries must remain employed out of necessity, industrialization and the adoption of new technologies along with labour-market mobility threaten much of the traditional work of older people. Development projects must ensure the participation of older people in income-generating opportunities and their eligibility for credit schemes (World Health Organization, 2002).

In developed countries, older workers are also facing challenges. During the 1980s and the 1990s, companies restructuring in OECD countries were much more likely to downsize than to expand employment and many sought to reduce the number of workers through early retirement for workers. In both public and private workplaces, downsizing, accompanied by early retirement, designed to give companies adjustment flexibility, has been common practice (Auer and Fortuny, 2000).

In recent years, the sustainability of these policies has come into question as concerns a rise over pension liabilities, mounting old-age dependency ratios, skills gaps and potential labour-force shortages (United Nations, 2007). Because people are living much longer, they potentially will be active for many more years than people were in previous generations. Mandatory retirement ages are artificially low considering the increase in lifespans and improvements in health. These changes have major implications for the labour force and the status of older workers (United Nations, 2006d).

Strong economic and social arguments can be made in support of reversing the early retirement trend in OECD countries. In the next 25 years, a further decline in employment rates and an increase in dependency rates will occur, as the number of persons at pensionable age will rise by 70 million while the working-age population will only grow by 5 million. Reversing the early retirement trend will prevent the employment ratio from falling (Auer and Fortuny, 2000). The pressures to eliminate mandatory retirement ages and extend the number of working years are increasing and the elimination of mandatory retirement ages has already occurred in several countries, such as Australia, New Zealand and the United States where workers are allowed to stay in the workforce as long as they are willing and able (United Nations, 2006d). Allowing knowledgeable, experienced and able persons to remain in the workplace will benefit employers and older persons alike. Many employers in these countries have recognized the value of retaining older workers and offer incentives for employees to remain on the job (Auer and Fortuny, 2000).

As people grow older, active ageing policies are necessary to allow older persons to remain in the labour force in accordance with their capacities and preferences. For individuals to remain productive and engaged in meaningful activity as they grow older, continuous training in the workplace and lifelong learning opportunities in the community are necessary (World Health Organization, 2002). For developing countries in particular, where only 50 per cent of adults over age 60 are literate, access to education and literacy early in life are critical for developing the skills that people will need in order to adapt and remain independent as they grow older (United Nations, 2002a). Low levels of education and illiteracy are associated not only with high rates of unemployment, but also with increased risks of disability and death for people as they age (World Health Organization, 2002).

Making the physical environment more accessible to older persons can mean the difference between dependence and independence. Public transportation must be made available and affordable, as it is critical for enabling older persons to participate in community life. Attention must also be given to environmental hazards such as insufficient lighting, absence of handrails and irregular walkways which can increase the risk of injury for older persons. In the workplace, older persons need training in new technologies, particularly in information technology, electronic communication and agriculture (ibid.). In the International Labour Office *World Employment Report, 1998-99: Employability in the Global Economy — How Training Matters* [12], it was argued that ongoing training was necessary throughout the working life of an individual to prevent the obsolescence of skills as persistent age discrimination had been reinforced by changes in work organization. Employers must ensure that education and training policies are adapted to the specific need of older workers. The better the education provided for older persons, the longer they will remain in employment (Auer and Fortuny, 2000).

In many cases, increased ageing worldwide has had a remarkable impact on family structures and roles as well as on labour patterns of other social groups examined in this chapter. For example, there are a growing number of health professionals migrating from developing countries to fill the increasing demand for long-term care for the ageing population in developed countries. This trend has resulted in the entry of more women into the labour market. While there is a benefit from the trend for sending countries in the form of increased remittances, there is also a loss of productive workers. Moreover, as population ageing increases in developing countries, older persons could be left without any family members to care for them (United Nations, 2006d).

Opening the world of work to persons with disabilities

The proportion of persons with disabilities in the global population at present is estimated to be at 10 per cent, which amounts to 650 million people (United Nations, 2006e). Given the phenomenon of global ageing and the prevalence of communicable diseases such as tuberculosis and HIV/AIDS, the incidence of disability will continue to increase.

Persons with disabilities are much more likely than those without disabilities to live in poverty, and of the 1.3 billion people surviving on less than $1 a day, persons with disabilities are often among the poorest (Albert, 2006). There is a strong correlation between poverty and disability, as people who are living in poverty are more likely to become disabled, and persons with disabilities are more likely to be poor (World Health Organization, 2004).

On 13 December 2006, the United Nations General Assembly adopted by consensus the Convention on the Rights of Persons with Disabilities (Assembly resolution 61/106; annex I) and the Optional Protocol to the Convention (annex II). For many people, this represents the promise of a new era, reflecting a significant shift in the discriminatory attitudes and practices that persons with disabilities have had to endure. The Convention will fill a gap in the international legal framework, and foster a paradigm shift leading to deep-rooted social change in the way that the situation of persons with disabilities is addressed.

More importantly, the Convention moves beyond the medical understanding of disabilities, that is to say, the understanding of what is wrong with someone, to a social understanding that recognizes disability as a limitation imposed upon individuals by social, cultural, economic and environmental barriers (Albert, 2006). It reaffirms that all persons with disabilities must enjoy all human rights and fundamental freedoms, and it clarifies and qualifies how all categories of rights apply to persons with disabilities.

Of the 650 million persons with disabilities, about 470 million are of working age. They are much more likely to be unemployed than persons without disabilities (International Labour Organization, 2006d). Workers with disabilities tend to fare less well than workers without disabilities, especially when unemployment rises. While discrimination is often a factor, another key cause is the inability to compete on the basis of relevant skills and qualifications (O'Reilly, 2004). For persons with disabilities to become self-reliant and more socially active, they need greater access to activities that give life meaning, and they must be integrated socially and economically into mainstream society. Institutional support to facilitate inclusion and empowerment requires the provision of access to education, training and recreation, and support for employment and social participation. Strategies must be developed to reduce discrimination against persons with disabilities that prevent access to all types of social opportunities (Metts, 2003).

Data availability on persons with disabilities in many countries is inadequate. However, it is clear that a large number of persons with disabilities who wish to secure employment remain unemployed. Disability significantly affects the participation rate, and low unemployment rates may point to a discouraged-worker effect where people do not enter the labour market because chances of finding employment are perceived to be low. The European Commission (2001) found that 14 per cent of the working-age population, approximately 26 million people, identified themselves as having a disability. Nearly 52 percent of persons with disabilities were economically inactive compared with 28 per cent of those without disability; and only 42 per cent of persons with disabilities were employed, compared with almost 65 per cent of those without disabilities. Other research found that during the 1990s, the unemployment rate of persons with disabilities of working age had been, on average, 80 per cent higher than that of people without disabilities (Organization for Economic Cooperation and Development, 2003).

Additionally, there is a clear relation between education and disability. In countries where data are available, on average, persons with disabilities have a lower educational level and fewer educational opportunities than persons without disabilities. As a result, persons with disabilities are less likely to attain the necessary qualifications to enter and compete in the labour market (European Commission, 2001).

The rate of employment of persons with disabilities is believed to be far lower in developing countries than in OECD countries. Yet, nearly 7 out of every 10 persons with disabilities live in developing countries. Ninety per cent of school-age children with disabilities in developing countries do not attend school, and the labour-market position of job-seekers with disabilities is dire. In most cases, there is no access to disability benefits or rehabilitation services (World Health Organization, 2003; United Nations Educational, Scientific and Cultural Organization, 2004). In Latin America, for example, there are roughly 85 million persons with disabilities, but only 2 per cent were reported as receiving adequate medical care (Pan American Health Organization, 2006). In the Asia-Pacific region, home to about 400 million persons with disabilities, the prevalence rates of disabilities across countries range from 0.7 to 20 per cent, with most living beneath the poverty line (Economic and Social Commission for Asia and the Pacific, 2006).

Considering the large numbers of persons with disabilities in the world, it will be impossible to achieve Millennium Development Goal 1 of cutting extreme poverty in half by 2015 if they are not brought into the development mainstream. Also, if Millennium Development Goals 2, , aiming to ensure that all children have access to primary education by the same year, is to be achieved then persons living with disabilities must be mainstreamed into the international development agenda.

Approaches to greater inclusion

Greater inclusion of persons with disabilities can be achieved through professional training. Training programmes that lead to recognized certification are essential for persons with disabilities who seek to gain employment. This type of training is going through a transition involving a shift from specialized institutions to mainstream programmes, open to all job-seekers. In many cases where persons with disabilities are being encouraged to enter mainstream training, physical inaccessibility as well as irrelevant courses, inadequate transportation and inflexibility of course design are often cited as reasons for their being unable to do so. Countries that have made progress in the mainstreaming of training are taking steps to deal with the barriers to participation mentioned above (O'Reilly, 2004).

Two approaches to inclusion and employment for workers with disabilities are sheltered employment, entailing a segregated environment for those whose needs do not allow for them to obtain employment in the open market, and supported employment. Supported employment developed as an alternative to traditional rehabilitation programmes, placing workers in integrated workplaces (ibid., 2004). A number of studies claim that supported employment has produced greater social and psychological benefits for persons with disabilities and have been more cost effective for the workers and taxpayers; however, the findings may be different in other countries (ibid, 2004).

Despite the large number of countries that have created employment quotas for persons with disabilities, the rates of compliance are generally low (Organization for Economic Cooperation and Development, 2003). Quota systems are based on the belief that without legislative intervention, the number of persons with disabilities in the workforce would be far lower than what it is at present. A number of countries that had not introduced quota systems decided instead to promote the voluntary approach to employment through improved vocational training and rehabilitation, and introduced anti-discrimination legislation to promote equal-opportunity employment. More than 40 countries have adopted antidiscrimination legislation, though there are some reports that such legislation has not been particularly useful or effective in promoting employment for persons with disabilities. More studies that examine the implementation and enforcement of anti-discrimination legislation in relation to employment are needed (O'Reilly, 2004).

Many Governments have recognized community-based rehabilitation (CBR) as an effective method for increasing community level activity aimed at the equalization of opportunities for persons with disabilities. Community-based rehabilitation aims to promote rehabilitation and social inclusion of persons with disabilities by allowing them to actively contribute to the development of their own communities. For these programmes to be successful, individual communities must take responsibility for addressing barriers to participation by all its members with disabilities. Organizations of persons with disabilities are a valuable resource through which to strengthen community-based rehabilitation programmes and should be given meaningful roles in their implementation and evaluation. As the participation of Disabled Persons Organization in community-based rehabilitation programmes increases, the number of persons with disabilities working in community-based rehabilitation programmes also increases, thus strengthening the involvement of persons with disabilities in the development of their own communities. Community-based rehabilitation programmes thus constitute important precursors of greater integration of persons with disabilities into the labour market (World Health Organization, International Labour Office and United Nations Educational, Scientific and Cultural Organization, 2004).

National Governments, non-governmental organizations and other stakeholders also have a critical role to play in community-based rehabilitation programmes. Approaches to implementation vary across countries but all programmes require support at the national level through policies, coordination and resource allocation. They also entail the recognition that all programmes should be based on a human rights approach, should reflect a willingness of the community to respond to the needs of persons with disabilities, and should involve motivated community workers who will form the core of community-based rehabilitation programmes (ibid.). There is a need to scale up these programmes which are typically found in communities with access to support services or communities where non-governmental organizations have worked to established them. These programmes need to be expanded to rural areas where access to health and social services is limited, as well as to large urban areas where many persons with disabilities are living in slums (ibid., 2004).

The global movement towards integration and greater participation has been championed by persons with disabilities, who are spurred on by increasing appreciation for the nature of disability as involving the interaction between impairments and the physical, social, and policy environments. Most important to the process of integrating persons with disabilities into mainstream society is combating the stigma and discrimination associated with having a disability. Removing discrimination in labour markets — and in the provision of social programmes such as health and education — is critical to overcoming these barriers.

Indigenous peoples: working from tradition to new challenges

For indigenous peoples, the challenge is not only how to achieve full employment and decent work, but also how to maintain their traditional occupations and lifestyles in a rapidly changing environment. They should be able to define and pursue their own visions of economic development, in the context of the adaptability and innovativeness of their cultures, their traditional knowledge and values, and their ancestral lands and resources.

It is difficult to define the "traditional occupations" of indigenous peoples accurately. They tend to have a strong collective element but the precise nature of particular occupations has changed significantly over time, adapting to needs, resources and technologies available to particular communities. Also, they have almost always been characterized by occupational pluralism, that is to say, the practising together of several activities in order to meet a community's subsistence needs. It is thus not only the activities themselves, but also the range of activities and their interrelationship characterizing the traditional occupations of indigenous peoples that contrasts with the situation in a "modern economy", which requires specialized labour and skills (Thomas, 2001). The growing inability to pursue their traditional occupations, owing to a changing global environment and the appropriation of ancestral lands, is a crucial contributing factor to the high incidence of poverty among indigenous peoples and is having detrimental effects on their cultures.

As a result, indigenous peoples are disproportionately represented among the poorest of society. Although indigenous peoples make up only 5 per cent of the world's population, they constitute about 15 per cent of the world's poorest (International Labour Organization, 2006e). Moreover, poverty in many Latin American countries tends to be deeper for indigenous people than for non-indigenous people, with the average incomes of indigenous poor people further below the poverty line (Hall and Patrinos, 2006).

The loss of control over traditional resource bases is also impacting on the culture of indigenous peoples. In particular, it has entailed the loss of traditional governance systems and customary laws for managing these resources as well as the loss of traditional knowledge of how to manage specific ecosystems. Whereas indigenous peoples traditionally place great emphasis on collectivism and mutual aid, integration into the mainstream economy, whether voluntary or involuntary, is leading to increased individualism. In addition to being adversely impacted by the reduced access to land, reciprocal ties are being further undermined by differential access to education, urbanization and the privatization of commonly held resources (Thomas, 2001).

The right of indigenous peoples to choose their form of economic development is reflected in article 5 of the United Nations Declaration on the Rights of Indigenous Peoples (United Nations, 2006f). Regrettably, this right is often not recognized. Indigenous peoples face considerable difficulties in finding employment in the mainstream economy. Although labour statistics are frequently not disaggregated by ethnicity, unemployment rates among indigenous peoples seem to be significantly higher than the national average in many countries.

Indigenous peoples face discrimination in all aspects of their lives: frequently considered to be underdeveloped, their traditions are not respected or they are denied citizenship on the basis of their ethnicity. This often hinders their access to education and employment (International Labour Organization, 2006e). Discrimination in the labour market is both a significant cause and a consequence of their poverty. In several Latin American countries, the portion of the difference in labour earnings between indigenous and non-indigenous people that is not explained by education level and other observable factors influencing productivity ranges from over one quarter to over one half. In addition, the average increase in earnings that derives from each year of additional schooling is slightly lower for indigenous peoples in four out five countries studied in Latin America. This gap between returns to education widens at higher education levels (Hall and Patrinos, 2006).

In addition to discrimination, inadequate education systems are the second key explanatory factor for the difficulties faced by indigenous peoples in obtaining employment. Both the quantity and quality of schooling obtained by indigenous peoples are typically insufficient. Indigenous children tend to have fewer years of schooling than non-indigenous children and their educational attainments are frequently low. Dropout, repetition and failure rates are high in indigenous schools. In some Latin American countries, the average education levels of indigenous people and non-indigenous people were represented by 2.3 and 3.7 years of schooling, respectively (ibid.). Since they frequently live in remote areas with poor infrastructure, indigenous children have difficulties accessing schools. In general, education services in indigenous areas are underfunded and poorly equipped with educational materials. In addition, formal education systems are mostly not well adapted to traditional ways of learning and the curriculum does not address the histories, knowledge, technologies and value systems of indigenous peoples. This type of education not only distances students from their own cultures but may also lead to low self-esteem and the feeling of being incapable of coping in the modern world (Thomas, 2001).

Little access to secondary and higher education is one of the main barriers to higher-skilled employment for indigenous peoples. Indigenous professionals thus tend to be significantly underrepresented in both the public and the private sectors. Scholarships, affirmative action programmes and distance education can be important means to facilitate access to further education. Those indigenous people who do succeed within the education system and achieve higher levels of education usually have to obtain that education in urban centres far removed from their communities. Returning to their communities is frequently problematic because of the few employment opportunities there that are suited to their skills.

Frequently, the disadvantages created through the schooling system are not offset by specific vocational training. Nevertheless, properly designed vocational training programmes that respond to the needs and priorities of indigenous peoples offer an important tool with which to enable participation on an equal basis in the labour market (International Labour Organization, 2006e).

When indigenous peoples do find employment, it is frequently in low-skilled jobs where the working conditions are often poor. Poor health, linked to malnutrition and inaccessibility of basic health services, frequently reduces their productivity and ability to find decent jobs. The fact that many indigenous peoples are not fluent in the national language and live in isolated and frequently inaccessible areas contributes to the problem. Debt bondage and other forms of forced labour practices frequently affect indigenous peoples (International Labour Organization, 2003b).

Although no comprehensive data on the magnitude of the problem exist, a series of cases and examples from all over the world indicate that indigenous children are disproportionately at risk in respect of child labour, particularly its worst forms. In Latin America, indigenous children are twice as likely to work as their non-indigenous peers (International Labour Organization, 2006e). In many indigenous communities, the concept of child labour is not well understood and not regarded as a serious problem. Although some forms of acceptable child work are linked to traditional beliefs and contribute to acquiring skills and knowledge, there is a need to identify the negative practices that contribute to child labour. In most cases, it is clearly not tradition, but a lack of alternatives, that leads indigenous children to undertake harmful and exploitative labour.

Despite the current serious employment situation of indigenous peoples, there is reason for hope. Over the past 10 years, issues affecting indigenous peoples have received increasing attention, owing in no small part to the accomplishments of the First International Decade of the World's Indigenous People (1995-2004) which are being consolidated through the undertakings of the second Decade (2005-2014). Also, discussions at the United Nations continue on the United Nations Declaration on the Rights of Indigenous Peoples. Some Governments have created employment programmes specifically targeted at indigenous peoples, which take their particular needs into account. Others have passed legislation guaranteeing bilingual education or have issued constitutional declarations against discrimination. These policies significantly improve labour-market prospects for indigenous peoples.

In some countries, the schooling gap between indigenous and non-indigenous peoples is narrowing — a prerequisite for indigenous people's having equal employment opportunities. However, discrimination must be overcome if differentials in labour earnings are to be eliminated.

Finally, new forms of employment are also providing opportunities for indigenous peoples. Business-creation initiatives, including tourism, managed by indigenous communities, offer the possibility of generating income and transmitting traditional knowledge while protecting ancestral lands. However, these initiatives should complement the development of existing industries in the community. The increasing awareness regarding the need to protect the intellectual and cultural property rights of indigenous peoples will hopefully also lead to the creation of new sources of income and employment for these people in the near future.

While these recent developments offer reason for hope, they should not be a cause for complacency. As seen above, many indigenous peoples continue to suffer from serious labour-market disadvantages. Providing them with concrete opportunities to pursue their economic development in line with their aspirations and needs constitutes an important step towards respecting indigenous rights, preserving traditional knowledge and promoting sustainable development.

Migrants and social disadvantage

International migration has become a central dimension of the globalization era, with implications for employment and unemployment. Stimulated by economic and social inequalities in the world, people are increasingly moving across borders in search of better opportunities. Legal migrants, with valuable skills, are generally able to secure attractive salaries and good working conditions, in health care, information technology, education and finance, which are among the fastest-growing industries. Illegal migrants, on the other hand, tend to take on low-skill jobs, even though they may be well educated, and to work under poor working conditions, mostly in agriculture, construction and household services. In certain cases, these working conditions may be in violation of labour laws of the host countries, as employers take advantage of the inability of illegal migrants to seek protection from the law.

The consequences of large-scale migration for social integration can be quite negative, including the separation of families for extended periods of time and the high risk of exploitation and discrimination faced by migrants. While migrants often benefit from the expanded work opportunities and higher remuneration in their destination countries, relative to origin countries, many face poor conditions of work and fill jobs that national workers reject or are not available for. Many migrants work in precarious and unprotected conditions in the growing informal economy. Work insecurity is particularly severe, with occupational accident rates being much higher for migrant workers.

In developed countries, migrant workers, particularly those obliged to seek low-status, lower-skill jobs, typically face a high degree of discrimination (Taran and Geronimi, 2003). Studies of ILO (2004c) suggest that in those countries more than one in three qualified immigrant applicants was unfairly excluded in job selection procedures. Migrants often have little or no means of legal protection against exploitation. They are more likely to be discriminated against in the workplace, as they often lack the language, negotiating and networking skills needed to enable them to fully capitalize on the opportunities offered in their destination countries. The tendency for migrants to be relegated to peripheral, low-skilled and low-paying work regardless of their achieved human capital subjects them and their families to social exclusion.

One of the most significant changes in migration patterns is increasing migration among women. Currently, the 95 million female migrants constitute half the international migrant population worldwide (United Nations, 2006b). Women migrants work mostly in low-status, low-wage production and service jobs and often in gender-segregated and unregulated sectors of the economy, mainly in domestic work. They are exposed to higher degree of exploitation, violence and trafficking.

In developed countries, there is no doubt that in a situation where the number of immigrants is rising, a strain is put on the labour market and social protection system. Even in some countries with a history of social solidarity and welfare protection, resentment towards immigrants has grown, linked to the high level of youth unemployment. Demands for greater assimilation, and for immigrants to learn the local language and history, usually represent coded expressions of hostility to people of other creeds, colour or appearance.

A pressing concern for many Governments is how to enable the growing international migrant streams to become better adapted into their receiving communities and countries. Policies for integrating migrants to the labour market, protecting their rights and preventing their exploitation are essential.

Concluding remarks

In all social groups, there has been a movement towards greater participation in the labour force around the world. Many groups are increasingly ready and able to engage in work, however defined. For the younger cohorts in society, there are indications that they are staying longer in education, and that fewer members of those cohorts are engaged in exploitative forms of child labour. Yet, while young people's entry into the labour force is delayed, their expectations are too often frustrated, paradoxically at a time when they are better prepared than ever before. At the other end of the age spectrum, older workers expect to stay longer within the labour force; sometimes this will be out of necessity, and often by choice.

On the other hand, the prospects for greater participation in the labour force have been much slower in materializing for persons with disabilities and indigenous peoples, who have traditionally been on the fringes of the labour market. While there are certainly hopeful signs that their rights and needs are being addressed, many challenges to greater participation of these groups remain.

It is in the area of gender where most progress for greater participation can be reported, but where at the same time, the largest inequalities among people have persisted. Too often, progress that allows for full and equal participation of women in the labour force has been set back by discrimination, leading to greater inequalities between women and men. A similarly mixed track record of progress and setbacks can be observed for migrants: while they have become an established (but underappreciated) part of the global workforce, their rights and needs still need much greater attention. These developments have reinforced inequalities, not only between these social groups and "mainstream society", but also among the groups themselves. This will be the topic of discussion in the next chapter.

Notes

[1] United Nations Statistics Division, Department of Economic and Social Affairs, "Progress towards the Millennium Development Goals, 1990-2005. Goal: Promote gender equality and empower women", available from *http://mdgs.un.org/unsd/mdg/Resources/Attach/Products/Progress2005/goal_3.pdf*.

[2] See International Labour Organization, "Decent work for women: ILO proposal to accelerate the implementation of the Beijing Platform for Action," International Seminar: Gender mainstreaming in Technical Cooperation Projects: for the labour and Social Spheres (St. Petersburg, 2000), available from *www.ilo.ru/other/event/gendsp2k/decwork1.pdf*.

[3] The decline in child labour is questioned by some critics who doubt the validity of the figures. It is argued that much child labour, particularly the hazardous forms, is invisible and that figures on child labour can be politically sensitive. Furthermore, no internationally agreed statistical definition of child labour currently exists and child labour will be in the agenda of the Eighteenth International Conference of Labour Statisticians in 2008.

[4] Despite the close link between poverty and child labour, the issue has received little attention in national development strategies, including poverty reduction strategies.

[5] Sixty-nine per cent of working children are engaged in agriculture (International Labour Organization, 2006b, figure I.3).

[6] However, many working children do not receive wages (Fyfe and Jankanish, 1997).

[7] Research on the relationship between child labour and youth employment, however, is scarce (International Labour Organization, 2006b).

[8] See General Assembly resolution 60/1.

[9] Ravallion and Wodon (2000) tested the effect of such an enrolment subsidy in rural Bangladesh and found that it increased schooling by far more than it reduced child labour, that is to say, the time spent at school partly came out of leisure.

[10] Seventy-seven per cent of children in Woodhead's study (1998) found that combining work and school was the best option in their current circumstances, with only 12 per cent preferring "school only".

[11] The United Nations definition of an ageing society is a country or region in which people aged 60 years or over constitute 10 per cent of the total population.

[12] Geneva, International Labour Organization, 1998.

Chapter IV

Inequalities, employment generation and decent work

The subject of inequality is central when examining the challenges of employment-generation and decent work (International Labour Organization, 2007). The evident worsening of economic and social inequality in the past three decades raises an important question on the impact, that such trends have had on the growth of employment and work opportunities. Although well-known economic models have postulated that some inequality promotes investment and economic growth, certain empirical evidence indicates that a high degree of inequality has a negative impact on subsequent economic outcomes. Moreover, better wealth redistribution can indeed promote sustainable economic growth which would generate a relative improvement in work opportunities for lower-income groups and for lower-income countries.

The present chapter begins by reviewing the trends and types of income inequalities. It then focuses on the labour-market and employment consequences of widening income inequality, looking at the direct effects of income inequality on economic outcomes. The chapter goes on to examine how non-economic inequalities affect economic outcomes and employment-generation. It is argued that a high degree of inequality tends to have a negative impact on subsequent economic outcomes and, in turn, on employment-generation and decent work.

Trends and types of economic inequalities

Increasing global economic inequalities and their social and economic consequences have been highlighted in several recent publications, notably *Report on the World Social Situation 2005*. (United Nations, 2005a). The share of the richest 10 per cent of the world's population has increased from 51.6 to 53.4 per cent of total world income (Bourguignon and Morrison, 2002). Also, the income gap between the richest and poorest countries has widened in recent decades (Berry and Serieux, 2006). In fact, the potential contribution of the global market during the 1980s and 1990s to growth and poverty reduction is still seriously under-realized in many developing countries (Osmani, 2003).

Functional distribution of income

Income inequality within many countries has been rising since the 1980s (Atkinson, 2003) after having decreased during the 1950s, 1960s and 1970s. The share of capital in total income has tended to rise while wages and worker benefits have tended to decline. This regressive shift in the functional distribution of income has occurred in both developed and developing countries. For example, one study (Harrison, 2002) found that within poorer countries, labour's share of income has been declining for some time, while the pace of decline has been increasing. In the richer countries too, labour's share of income is also falling; the Bank for International Settlements has shown that wages as a share of national income in the rich G10 countries have been on a downward trend since 1980, having fallen from about 63 to below 59 per cent in 2006.

Low incomes in labour markets do reflect low productivity to some extent, but not always, as can be seen in the divergent trends of productivity and real wages in the United States of America, where productivity has risen, while wages fell between 2001 and 2005. Indeed, policymakers can try to raise productivity and should do so, just as employers can be expected to want to do so; but policymakers can also look more attentively at non-productivity factors that cause workers to have low earnings, such as the pervasive practice of middlemen or landlords, or simply relatives, of taking away part of their incomes, and the practice of using worker indebtedness to induce compliance with dismally low wages.

Above all, policymakers can introduce laws and regulations to facilitate stronger bargaining power of, or on behalf of, workers, so that workers themselves can secure higher wages and benefits that correspond to their productivity. Strengthening of collective bargaining may also be a powerful force for higher productivity. It is too often forgotten that collective bargaining carried out by institutions and groups has a positive effect on dynamic efficiency, especially where those doing the bargaining have a vested interest in the preservation of the productive activity for the longer term. This is a positive externality of trade unions that has been overlooked by critics concentrating on their alleged effect on wages and labour "rigidities".

This regressive shift in the functional distribution of income is also partly a reflection of the forces unleashed by globalization, with a greatly increased abundance of labour supply on the one hand and a greater mobility of capital on the other. The abundant globalized labour supply contributes to keeping down wages: employers can always impose a pay cut merely by threatening to shift production to lower-income countries. This has fuelled the growth of functional income inequality. This global labour supply that is in surplus is acting very much like an unlimited labour surplus holding down real wages as economic growth proceeds. In effect, for many groups of workers in developed countries in particular, real wages have not been rising at all and have even declined in some countries, while the returns to capital have been rising. This is an issue of capital mobility rather than of factor productivity, reflected by a prolonged process of concession bargaining that has reduced real wages and curbed benefits to workers. Several studies have indeed attributed the decline in labour's share in part to financial liberalization (Harrison, 2002; Lee and Jayadev, 2005).

Globalization of financial markets makes it more difficult to tax the relatively mobile factors of production such as capital (Wachtel, 2003). In effect, taxation on capital has been falling, while the effective tax share borne by labour income has been rising, further worsening the functional income distribution.

Governments are advised to consider ways of checking the growth of inequality in order to preserve social cohesion and create a favourable environment for sustained economic growth. One way to accomplish this would be to find ways of redistributing factor incomes, (without undermining the incentive structures excessively) so that the growing functional inequality is not reproduced in personal inequality. Governments must begin by recognizing that there is no prospect of labour markets' adjusting in such a way as to reduce the functional inequalities.

Wage differentials

The growth of overall income inequality has also been attributed to the growth of wage differentials. The real wages of manual workers (unskilled labour) have fallen relative to the wages and salaries of relatively educated and skilled workers.

Trade openness, among several relevant factors, has contributed to the wider wage differential by favouring the wages of workers in export sectors and increasing the earnings of skilled labour relative to unskilled labour (Hoekman and Winters, 2005). Empirical studies have shown that increased trade openness has increased wage inequality in a number of Latin American countries (Milanovic and Squire, 2005; Pavcnik and others, 2002; Beyer, Rojas and Vergara, 1999; Attanasio, Goldberg and Pavcnik, 2003; Harrison and Hanson, 1999). In those cases, the opportunities opened up by the forces of globalization have not reached the poorest groups since the expansion of employment is related to a level of skills that the poor do not possess. Thus, growth has a highly unequal distribution which is increasing; this creates the class of the working poor or perpetuates their existence. However, in other regions, like that of the East Asian countries, the expansion of manufactured exports has brought higher employment and a subsequent increase in real wages, thereby reducing income inequality. For instance, in Malaysia, the demand for unskilled labour created by the process of export-led industrialization has increased considerably and has raised wages for unskilled workers (Jomo, 2006).

Trade liberalization in the absence of other policies will not necessarily lead to higher growth and may even decrease welfare in the shortrun (van der Hoeven and Lubker, 2006). Complementary policy measures have to be in place to counter any short-term negative effect of trade liberalization. For instance, in East Asian countries, greater investment in secondary and tertiary schooling has reduced the negative impact of trade liberalization by preventing a direct translation of educational inequalities into skill-based ones. This observation suggests the need to combine an important social policy with an economic one.

Foreign direct investment (FDI) by multinational enterprises has tended to raise wages in the modern industrial sector in developing countries, but also to widen wage differentials between regions, with strong gains being made by areas in which export-oriented activities are concentrated, leaving other regions behind, and within those local labour markets attracting FDI, with foreign firms paying much more than local firms in the same sectors. Wage differentials between multinational enterprises and local firms may not reflect only skill or productivity differentials. Firm-level data have shown that relatively high wages paid by multinational enterprises may induce a form of labour-market creaming and the emergence of a special labour-market dualism. Spillover benefits have been found to be greater where the multinational enterprises are in a competitive market involving local firms and when the technological and productivity differences between multinational enterprises and local firms are not substantial (Moran, Graham and Blomstrom, 2005).

The offshoring of jobs may also be widening wage differentials, within the countries "losing" jobs and within those "gaining" jobs. The transfer of jobs, and the threat to transfer them, may affect wage differentials as well as labour's share of gross national product (GNP). Traditionally, many of the jobs being transferred from developed to developing countries have been relatively low-wage manual jobs, and the threat to transfer more jobs led to a decline in wages for workers in such jobs in the developed countries. Now, however, the transfer has shifted to services, including a range of professional services, and offshoring has begun to affect wage differentials in developed countries by squeezing the middle-income groups of service workers. Several examples in the United States of America and Germany as well as United Kingdom of Great Britain and Northern Ireland (and almost certainly elsewhere) show that wage differentials between the high-paid and low-paid have grown partly because of the erosion of wage earnings of the middle-income groups (Autor, Katz and Kearney, 2006), precisely those most affected by offshoring and the threat of offshoring of jobs.

There is also the role of economic shocks, which have grown in number and intensity in the recent past. While globalization in itself has been boosting wage inequality between and within countries, economic shocks in themselves also seem to generate increases in wage inequality by disturbing inertias that characterize all labour markets. A case in point was Indonesia's economic crisis of the late 1990s, in the course of which real wages of manual workers had fallen sharply and stayed low when wages of other groups recovered (Dhanani and Islam, 2004).

Casualization, contractualization and wage differentiation

One form of wage inequality, which is made worse when seen in terms of social income (that is to say, when income is measured in terms of wages plus non-wage benefits), is that between those in regular, formal jobs and those in casual, informal jobs. While there has been a growth of casualization and of the number of workers in casual work statuses, there is some evidence that the differentials between the incomes of those in the several work statuses have been wide and are widening.

In developed countries, there has been a shift to more temporary employment, particularly through agency employment. In the United Kingdom of

Great Britain and Northern Ireland, for instance, it has been found that male temporary workers received wages that were 16 per cent lower than those of their male counterparts with similar skills and other personal characteristics who were regular workers, and that female temporaries received 13 per cent less than their equivalents in regular employment (Booth, Francesconi and Frank, 2002). Another study found that agency workers received 9 per cent less pay than other workers with similar characteristics (Forde and Slater, 2005). There and elsewhere in country members of the Organization for Economic Cooperation and Development (OECD), temporary workers do much worse in terms of entitlements and access to benefits such as holidays and pensions (Organization for Economic Cooperation and Development, 2002).

In Australia, where casual employment has risen sharply over the past quarter of a century, casual workers typically receive much lower pay, even though there has been a formal practice of casual loading (providing a premium for workers with casual status). Often the lower pay is due to an absence of bonuses and to the practice of putting casuals on lower classification levels (Campbell, 2004).

In the United States, agency temporary workers earn less than others doing similar jobs, even though their wages may actually be higher than the average for similar labour. The main reason is that the temporaries typically receive entitlement to fewer enterprise benefits and lower-value benefits when they do have entitlement to them. They commonly lack health-care coverage, employment insurance, retirement pay and vacation allowances. The same pattern emerges in Japan (Gottfried, Nishiwara and Aiba, 2006; Weathers, 2001).

In developing countries, where casual labour is almost the norm, as the informal sector tends to be large, one must take note of the fact that it is continuing to spread and that those engaged in casual labour earn much less than those in regular employment and often work without any social benefits. For instance, in the State of Gujarat in India, casual workers were earning much less than those doing regular jobs of a similar nature and less than those nominally self-employed (Unni and Rani, 2002).

The trend of casualization is accompanied by contractualization, as standard collective contracts are being increasingly replaced by individualized contracts based on bargaining between employers and employees. In the process, workers' bargaining power has been eroded, especially for those with lower skill levels. At the same time, an individual worker's ability to bargain becomes more important than before in determining wages, resulting in greater differentiation of wages among workers and worsening income distribution.

In sum, casualization and contractualization have been a means of lowering social income. This trend has further re-enforced wage differentials among workers.

Migrants and the native-born

Growing labour migration will also have strong effects on wage levels, wage differentials and access to social services. Some observers believe the effect of migration on wages in areas of in migration is limited because of labour-market segregation. For example, a study by the World Bank (2006) claimed that in the mid-1990s as many as 70 per cent of recent migrants from developing to developed countries had been in jobs that non-migrants preferred to avoid. Wolf (2006) argues that the notion that immigrants are working at jobs that natives are unwilling to take is erroneous on two counts. First, the supply of labour is dependent on its price. Without immigrants, people would have to spend more on nannies, cleaners, farm workers and so on. Second, most of the workers doing the jobs also performed by immigrants are actually native-born. The obstacle, it seems, is not the absence of native-born workers, but the fact that they would have to be paid higher wages if immigrants were absent.

Clearly, the macroeconomic effects are complex. Raising the supply of labour willing to work for low wages and without non-wage benefits may encourage the growth of production based on labour-intensive technologies using relatively unskilled labour; but this would deter process innovation that would boost productivity, which is what ultimately .raises national income, growth and ultimately employment. Thus, while widening wage differentials through the boosting of the labour supply at the lower-skilled end may help individual employers, it could harm economic growth and dynamism.

Minimum wages

Throughout the twentieth century, an important weapon for combating poverty and income insecurity was the statutory minimum wage. With increasing globalization, it has come under attack led by the international financial agencies and some employer organizations. The critics have claimed that minimum wages priced low-productivity workers out of employment and created price distortions that affected the whole wage structure to the detriment of employment-creation and national competitiveness.

The arguments for and against minimum wages have been reviewed extensively (see, for example, Standing, 2002). Perhaps the best argument for them is that they can set a standard for decent work and guide collective and individual bargaining. However, their effectiveness in flexible labour markets characterized by economic openness and widespread non-standard and informal labour relations is limited. Some observers believe a statutory minimum wage does tend to raise "wages" in the informal economy (Devereux, 2005), although enforcement is likely to be very weak in such spheres.

While statutory minimum wages have been eroded by legislative reforms in many countries, a few countries have moved in the other direction. The United Kingdom of Great Britain and Northern Ireland introduced a national minimum wage for the first time in 1997, and the Governments of several countries have extended the coverage of their minimum wage system to groups of workers that were excluded. For example, South Africa extended its coverage to domestics and farm labourers in 2001, China to domestics in 2003, and Bolivia to agricultural workers in 2005. Nevertheless, these are exceptions with respect to the international trend.

The reality in developing countries and in flexible labour markets almost everywhere is that a statutory minimum wage is extremely hard to enforce. Moreover, many Governments have tended to bow to pressures to weaken their universality. Across the world, with a few exceptions, the value of the minimum wage has been allowed to fall relative to average wages and relative to basic subsistence income levels.

Very often, employers have been allowed to pay lower wages to young workers, and often part-time workers and casual workers are excluded from coverage. Frequently, differential minima have been introduced, creating administrative complexity and, paradoxically, leaving the most vulnerable least protected.

This problem is compounded by lack of awareness. Surveys in a large number of developing countries have found that many workers, particularly the poorest and most insecure, are unaware of the existence of a minimum wage, and even when they are aware, do not have the capacity to demand it.

In sum, the minimum wage has been a blunt instrument for providing income security for workers, and this is particularly the case in developing countries. It does have value, but not too much should be expected of it, particularly as a means of combating poverty and economic insecurity owing to exclusion in terms of coverage and difficulties in enforcement.

Impact of inequalities on employment and decent work

Given the global trend of increased inequality, the central question is whether or not the growth in inequality has tended to slow the growth of employment and work opportunities. Although certain economic models have postulated that some inequality promotes investment and economic growth, several empirical studies suggest that inequality lowers subsequent growth. Inequality in income and wealth can indeed reduce the possibilities of overall growth, with negative consequences for employment-creation and decent work. It seems, then, that some income redistribution can have a positive impact on employment outcomes, although the connections between inequality and economic development are still unclear. The argument for reducing inequality is further supported by the linkage between inequality and the perpetuation of poverty, as measured in terms of income and wealth as well as access to productivity — enhancing social services such as education and health (United Nations, 2005a).

Although economists have long believed that there is a trade-off between economic efficiency and social justice, empirical observations show that they are not incompatible and that inequality can have even a negative effect on subsequent economic outcomes. Some recent development theories would even argue that sustainable economic growth and productivity depend on the widest distribution of wealth, health and better education.

There is an important relationship between inequality and the rate of savings that will affect the rate of growth of a closed economy in the long run. Inequalities, moderate or high, in income distribution concentrate money in the hands of those who are willing to save (considering that as income increases, the marginal savings rate increases[1]), accumulate and invest, thereby boosting the growth rate. This consideration has been used to deter government efforts at redistributive taxation.

There are opposing views as well, arguing that under specific circumstances, a certain degree of redistribution can actually enhance savings and push up

growth rates. From one perspective, contrary with the standard model of economic growth, savings behaviour is determined not only by income, but by
investment and aspirations, and those aspirations are affected by existing inequalities of income and wealth. In an extremely poor country, redistributive
policies may bring down the rate of savings and therefore the rate of growth in
the medium or even long run. The choice is difficult: an egalitarian policy
devised to reduce deprivation and inequality in poor countries is necessary, but
at the same time it can bring down the rate of savings and consequently the rate
of growth. In medium-income countries, however, the story is different. Redistributive policies may generate more savings at the national level, because they
create a middle class with aspirations to a better economic life in the long term.
A redistribution policy would give the opportunity to increase their rate of savings to those who could not otherwise afford to do so.

An argument directed against the standard "inequality enables savings,
investment and economic growth" model can also be put forth, based on effective demand. If redistribution indeed lowers domestic savings, it increases
effective demand in the national market, since the flip side of lower savings is
higher consumption. Such inequality-reducing redistributive policies would
increase effective demand for goods and services, thus spurring economic
growth, especially when domestic investment was not constrained by domestic
savings. Furthermore, income determines not only the level of consumption,
but also the pattern of composition. At low levels of income, the needs for
food, clothing and shelter are more important. Therefore, an income change in
favour of the poor and the middle class, through economic growth or redistributive policies, opens up new consumption possibilities that are more likely to
be skewed towards labour-intensive and domestically produced goods and services, compared with the consumption pattern of the rich. This shift in consumption structure would be more favourable to economic growth owing to its
stimulating effect on the domestic economy. At the same time, this will have
further impact on the redistribution of income, as the new demand by con-
sumers will set up derived demand for factors of production and create a relative improvement in work opportunities for lower-income groups, thereby setting in motion a virtuous circle of growth and reduced inequality. Thus, the
composition of product demand resulting from a given level of inequality
influences both the functional and the personal distribution of income. There

is no necessary cause-and-effect relationship between redistributive policy and slower economic growth.

Another macroeconomic implication of inequality is associated with the imperfection of credit markets, a typical characteristic of unequal societies. Although the access to credit by the poorest groups will not affect the creation of employment in a massive way, access to entrepreneurship can alleviate poverty and reduce unemployment. In this way, there will be a change in the supply and demand for labour and, consequently, in the wage rate. The shift of people to an entrepreneurial activity will raise their income and the income of the remaining workers would rise as well, because of the resulting upward pressure on wages. In other words, the market equilibrium is inefficient under high inequality; there are alternative solutions that can improve the situation of some individuals without hurting anyone else. The lack of access to credit creates inefficiency in the economy as a whole. Therefore, less inequality with a more efficient credit market will improve the efficiency of the economy, raising the level of employment and work conditions.

In sum, the long-held preconception that redistributive policies necessarily retard economic growth and thus employment-creation needs to be challenged on many grounds. In the context of securing decent work for all, social and economic policies aimed at reducing inequality have an important role to play, especially under circumstances where inequality is extremely high and in middle-income countries.

Socio-political inequality, economic growth and employment generation

Full employment and decent work require more than just economic inputs: human and social capital is also essential. Income and social inequalities create a deficit in human and social capital detrimental to employment generation. Further, the goal of full employment and decent work cannot be achieved unless equality of opportunity and access to basic social services are ensured. *Report on World Social Situation 2005* (United Nation, 2005a) found that inequalities in education access and outcomes, health status, and other dimensions of human capital are pervasive and growing in many societies. The present section explores the way socio-political factors negatively affect economic growth and employment-generation, primarily through the impact on human and social capital.

Gender inequality undermines growth and employment-creation

As discussed in chapter III, women are overrepresented in the informal economy where jobs are lower-paying and less stable, and the rights of workers less protected. With few exceptions, women earn less than men in all employment categories. Although women's opportunities to participate in the labour force have expanded in recent decades, and there has been a decline in inequality between men and women in many countries, women's access to paid employment remains lower than that of men in most of the developing world, and there is evidence that inequality among women is increasing.

Gender inequality and discrimination are incompatible with decent work. In addition, gender inequality impacts economic outcomes ultimately, and employment-generation and decent work in other ways as well. For one, women spend a higher percentage of their income on feeding and educating children (United Nations Children's Fund, 2005). In fact, the effect of mother's income on child survival is nearly 20 times that of the father's (Boeri, del Boca and Pissarides, 2005). Therefore, where gender inequality is high, there are likely to be fewer resources invested in human capital, limiting future growth. Also, income inequality reinforces educational disparities between women and men which, in turn, contribute to continuing inequality. Gender discrimination in employment also results in an inefficient use of human capital: when hiring decisions are made based on factors irrelevant to the task, such as sex of the applicant, women are systematically marginalized and their human capital investment goes to waste, undermining economic growth and thus the goal of decent work for all.

Health as human development

The link is well established between the health status of a population and economic growth and prospects for employment-generation as well as achieving decent work for all. The health of a population can affect the level of productivity; therefore, good health is essential for a productive labour force. There is also evidence that the health of a population affects the level of foreign direct investment (FDI) because foreign firms are less likely to invest in countries where people have poor health. FDI flows are positively correlated with life expectancy and negatively correlated with HIV prevalence (International Labour Organization, 2005).

HIV reduces the quality and quantity of labour through the loss of human capital and through direct losses of the labour force in AIDS-related mortality. In many poor countries, the health and education sectors are losing a large number of personnel owing to AIDS-related deaths, thereby limiting capacity to build future human capital. HIV/AIDS is particularly devastating because it hits the working-age population hardest. High turnover and absenteeism among skilled labour, due to HIV/AIDS-related mortality and illness, cut profit and discourage investment in many countries. This is particularly the case in sub-Saharan Africa.

Hunger prevents development of human capital

Hunger and its manifestations negatively impact the labour force through low-ered human capital and productivity. It is also well documented that hungry and malnourished children face particular challenges to learning (World Food Programme, 2006). Hunger affects both an individual's capacity to learn through its effects on brain development and a person's ability to take advantage of learning opportunities in school.

Lack of nutrients during pregnancy and in infancy can lead to irreversible damage to the structure and size of the brain. Low birth weight also has lasting implications for future cognitive ability and academic performance. "Growth faltering" describes the failure of young children to grow to their full potential. In developing countries, as many as one out of three children under age 5 exhibits stunted growth. Stunting can lead to cognitive impairment.

Hungry children have reduced school attendance and enrolment, and they are more likely to drop out. When in school, hungry children have a difficult time concentrating and have shorter attention spans. Hunger also has negative effects on learning for adults, who in addition to suffering the long-term effects of hunger in childhood also experience lower productivity associated with low caloric intake, as well as lower concentration, poorer attendance in work and school and impaired mental functioning (ibid.).

Racial and ethnic minorities and human capital

Racial and ethnic minorities and migrant groups are often subject to social and economic exclusion through labour market discrimination and in terms of access to public goods such as education and health care (Gradstein and Shiff, 2006). Racial/ethnic discrimination commonly results in an unequal distribution of resources across ethnic groups and in some countries ethnicity and income are highly correlated.

Though some argue that ethnic disparities in income are due to human capital differences between ethnic groups, there is significant evidence that suggests that the ethnic differences in occupational attainment and income go well beyond education and skill differentials, and that in fact, ethnic minorities do not receive the same return to education and skills in the labour market as do members of the dominant group owing to discrimination (Frickey, Murdoch and Primon, 2006; Coopersmith, 2006; Berthoud, 2000; Lee, 2004).

The existence of ethnic discrimination and income disparities weakens social cohesion further. In its Declaration, the World Conference against Racism, Racial Discrimination, Xenophobia and Related Intolerance, held in 2001 in Durban, South Africa, affirmed that racism and racial discrimination "are among the root causes of many internal and international conflicts, including armed conflicts, and the consequent forced displacement of populations" (United Nations, 2001). Given that disparities in income can lead to violent conflict, it is not surprising that a large number of the violent conflicts in the world in recent years have had an ethnic component (Gurr, 1993, 2000).

Empirical studies show that ethnic discrimination in the labour market is pervasive and persists despite policies directed against it (Fugazzo, 2003). Discrimination can take the form of negative stereotypes regarding ethnic minorities' work capacities, can be transferred intergenerationally through lower social and human capital, and can occur at the institutional or systematic level. For example, when job opportunities are not advertised, but shared only by word of mouth, ethnic minorities with less social capital are less likely to be aware of such positions and to apply for them. Along similar lines, although the requirements of testing and/or professional certification may appear to treat all applicants equally, in reality qualified ethnic minorities might find it difficult to acquire those credentials owing to remoteness of locations and/or language disadvantages.

When employment decisions are based on irrelevant factors such as race or ethnicity, or the full pool of potential applicants is not considered, not only does discrimination infringe on the human rights of ethnic minorities, but it also constitutes an inefficient use of human capital.

Income inequality is detrimental to
human development and social cohesion/trust

Though research results in recent years have been mixed, the latest research based on the best available data finds a consistent relationship between income inequality and health quality (Ram, 2006). It is not just individual income or employment that affects people's health and well-being. Aggregate levels of unemployment and income inequality are also associated with poorer health in the community. There is a strong body of research that links low income to such health indicators as mortality rates, malnutrition and stunted growth, HIV prevalence and general poor health (International Labour Organization, 2005; Ram, 2006; World Food Programme, 2006).

The relative income hypothesis posits that an individual's health is affected by the distribution of income within a society through inequality's effects on social and human capital. According to this perspective—which has mixed empirical support—in very unequal societies, there tends to be less investment in public goods because they are seen as subsidies from the wealthy to the poor. For example, the fact that there tends to be less investment in public education and health care and a greater use of private services among the wealthy in essence cuts off the poor from opportunities to improve their human capital and stay healthy.

Income inequality also affects economic growth through its effect on education. The relationship between education and income inequality is complex and reciprocal. Limited labour-market opportunities in high-inequality countries influence the decisions of boys and girls on enrolment in school through the associated lack of incentive to stay in school. Moreover high levels of inequality associated with poverty often mean that children, especially girls, are taken out of school to help with household duties or to contribute to household income through paid work. The resultant lower educational attainment, in turn, further fuels income disparities.

Numerous studies link educational enrolment to socio-economic status. Cross-national studies find a large gap in educational attainment achieved by students in the top 20 per cent compared with those in the bottom 40 per cent of the income distribution (Buchmann and Hannum, 2001).

Increasing educational attainment can also increase income inequality. In the United States, there is evidence that increases in income inequality are at least partly attributable to the increasing returns to college degrees, as graduates make more than non-graduates. As the number of college graduates increases, income inequality increases (Lemieux, 2006). At the same time, weakening unions and declining real minimum wages have lowered incomes for non-college graduates. There is also evidence that the education-based wage gap can be reduced through on-the-job training (Hamil-Luker, 2005).

The relationship is complicated further by recent studies showing that returns to primary education in developing countries may be overestimated, particularly when labour-market conditions are not taken into consideration (McKenzie, 2006; Fryer and Vencatachellum, 2005). Where the class structure is rigid, education is likely to have less impact on income inequality. Also, there is some evidence that education is more important in determining occupational attainment for the middle class—which is often small in countries with high income inequality—than for the poor or wealthy. For the poor and the wealthy, intergenerational transfer of occupational status is much more likely. Recent cross-national studies find that public education expenditures reduced the level of income inequality in countries over time (Rudra, 2004; Sylwester, 2000). This relationship was found to be stronger in OECD countries where class structure is arguably less rigid and poverty less extreme. Another study found that economic liberalization may limit the effects of secondary enrolment on income equalization (Wells, 2006).

Social cohesion and political stability are important for economic stability, investment and growth and, ultimately, for the health of the labour market and employment opportunities and conditions. Income inequality can compromise social cohesion, lead to political violence and endanger government stability. In other words, income inequality contributes to a political and social environment that is not conducive to decent work and full employment.

There is also a correlation between income inequality and measures of social capital such as generalized trust. In countries where income inequality is higher, there is less general trust of others. Trust is an important factor in economic growth, as uncertainty is linked to lower investment. Where there is less inter-personal trust, individuals are apt to be less likely to enter into the agreements with each other that are essential for economic development. Where there is a high degree of social cohesion, transaction costs are lowered owing to higher levels of trust and social capital, and lowered transaction costs are conducive to thriving economic activity. Income inequality breaks the bonds of trust and therefore lowers social cohesion. Ultimately, lowered social cohesion strains institutions and impedes growth, which negatively impacts labour-market conditions and is likely to further fuel income inequality (Easterly, Ritzan and Woolcock, 2006).

Income inequality can generate discontent and grievances among the population, particularly when people observe a discrepancy between what they believe is right or fair and the current situation in which they live. When the government is perceived as complicit in the inequality, such grievances may be aimed towards the government and manifest themselves in a variety of ways ranging from conventional political participation (that is to say, in democracies, voting for candidates supportive of redistribution or other policies aimed at addressing the inequality) to protests and, in some cases, even political violence. In fact, cross-national empirical research generally finds that income inequality can lead to political violence (Lichbach, 1989; Schock, 1996). There is evidence that political violence is more likely to result from economic inequality when the State is weak, in other words, when it is unable to maintain order effectively and/or deliver goods and services to the population (Schock, 1996). Therefore, developing countries with weaker State institutions are more susceptible to violence resulting from income inequality.

Finally, democracy and the economic freedom it entails are also important for decent work and full employment. The relationship between income inequality and political violence suggests that democracies may not emerge or may be unable to survive if severe inequalities are not addressed. There is a general consensus that the middle class is important for democracy, and that while there is not a perfect relationship between the two, high income inequality generally means a small middle class. Some research finds a direct relationship between income inequality and democracy, though the findings are disputed (Muller, 1995; Bollen and Jackman, 1995).

Policy directions

Policies and strategies to promote and generate full employment and decent work should take into account the issue of inequality, as there are linkages between inequalities and the achievement of full employment and decent work. Addressing economic, social and political inequalities that underlie labour-market performance as well as the corresponding impact of the labour market on inequalities should underpin policy considerations. Taking these synergies and compensating mechanisms into account is therefore essential in developing policy packages and in shaping political support.

The design and choice of policy strategies directed towards reducing inequalities while promoting job creation will have to take into account, first and foremost, the specific level of development of different countries and the varied motivations for redistribution. Factors that affect the growing inequality and rising unemployment will have to be considered in the policy design, including redistributive policy involving such elements as changes in taxation and benefit systems, labour-market conditions, the changing demographic structure of the population, the changing social structures and human rights.

Redistributive policies

Macroeconomic policies designed to address growing income inequality and rising unemployment should weigh the advantages of progressive taxation and government social spending which often serve to supplement income sources of the poor and the working poor. However, grants of tax relief as a means of promoting employment can reduce overall tax revenues and result in lower spending on education, training, health care and other social services needed by the poor. It is important, therefore, that the adverse impact on social spending of tax relief programmes be weighed against the gains in employment-creation.

In addition, the macroeconomic effect of reducing inequalities, which can lead to a shift in demand towards goods and services needed by the poor, should be assessed as a means of opening employment opportunities for lower-income groups.

Wealth redistribution strategies, such as land reform and estate/inheritance taxation, should be more widely implemented and enforced to promote access to land and other productive assets. Success in land reform is often a long-term process and requires mechanisms to support the growth and stability of incomes derived from the land. Otherwise, land recipients can end up utilizing the land as collateral against loans, with failure to repay those loans eventually leading to loss of land ownership.

The deepening of inequality as a result of the various economic crises in the past decades offers important lessons. In particular, the disproportionate costs borne by the poor when economic programmes fail — in terms of hunger, loss of health-care services and reduction in educational opportunities — and the disproportionate benefits gained by the rich when economic programmes succeed should be rectified in policy designs that promote full employment and decent work. Ethical arrangements and fair allocation of risk lead to improved social harmony and socially optimal allocation of resources and minimize perverse risk-taking. In addition, a social risk management perspective needs to be incorporated in policies to ensure that the poor and working poor — who are least capable of absorbing shocks — are provided with appropriate social safety nets.

Labour-intensive initiatives that provide more employment opportunities for the poor should be pursued by Governments. For instance, the employment impact of public infrastructure projects can be enhanced by utilizing labour-intensive production methods and by promoting public works programmes if they are deemed appropriate given limited resources. Another example is the promotion of small and medium-sized enterprises which typically utilize labour-intensive technologies.

Labour-market policies
The policies that promote job creation and entrepreneurship through either tax or customs duties incentives (such as industrial zones) should consider the relative abundance of labour vis-à-vis capital in most of the developing world, that is to say, incentives should be structured consistent with the relative supply of labour and capital.

When seeking to attract foreign investments, Governments together with other countries, should ensure that the intercountry competition does not lead to a "race to the bottom" by compromising domestic standards on living wages and safe working conditions, and the granting of incentives to enterprises that may reduce government revenues and lead to lower spending on social services, health care and education for society at large. Regional cooperation in this regard may serve as an effective countervailing bargaining force vis-à-vis corporations and commercial interests whose size may dwarf those of small developing economies. In addition, the role of trade unions in strengthening collective bargaining can be harnessed in the negotiation process.

Minimum wage policies need to incorporate the minimum cost of living and geographical differences in respect of labour supply, living standards and costs of doing business. Furthermore, government incentives to businesses should take into account various aspects of investment and not solely wages. Other incentives would include government investments in human capital and infrastructure, the streamlining of licensing requirements, good governance and the stability and reliability of legal systems.

The lack of regulatory oversight in the informal economy exposes its workers to greater risk of abuse, poor working conditions and lack of benefits. Policies on work formalization that would provide social security benefits and legal protection to workers need to be carefully balanced against the demand for less formal arrangements often typically associated with start-up and entrepreneurial activities. Conditions for any exception need to be laid out and must ensure that the largest enterprises, well past start-up stages, are required to formalize their workforce. It is therefore imperative that policies weigh the pros and cons of formalization.

The increasing practice of casualization of workers, while indeed allowing for the "distribution" of part-time work among potential workers, does not create an environment conducive to worker advancement, retention of skills and long-term productivity gains.

The design of policies to promote employment and decent work also needs to incorporate the demographic and social changes in society, such as the growth in the number of youth and older people, the growth of households headed by single-women, the displacement of indigenous peoples from their former environments of survival. For example, policies that do not take into account the number of older people as well as the increasing proportion of youth could create biases against these workers, thereby not only generating increasing unemployment in these age cohorts of the population, but also disregarding the higher productivity that older workers may offer to society. Similarly, policies that fail to account for the growing number of household headed by single women, could fail to increase women's employment though, inter alia, not providing childcare and family health benefits.

Low-skilled workers and the working poor would benefit from investments in human capital undertaken to bridge the inequalities in opportunities. Programmes that provide skills development through education and training will help entry-level workers advance. Initiatives towards strengthening entrepreneurial skills and innovative practices could promote the creation of sustainable enterprises and improve job quality.

Political and legal reforms

Policies on employment and decent work should factor in political and legal reforms to ensure that such initiatives do not exacerbate inequalities in society and that they provide employment opportunities for all and protect the rights of workers.

Giving voice to all members of society, including workers and the unemployed, women, migrants and other marginalized groups, should ensure that their views on matters affecting their lives are heard. Democratic societies, with their laws and legislation already in place, often fall short in terms of those laws' implementation and this problem should be addressed. In other countries where such laws are absent, taking into account the views and opinions of workers, the unemployed and the marginalized can lead to a more effective design and implementation of strategies; and allowing for public reviews of proposed policies and programmes, wherein views and conflicting perspectives could be solicited and better addressed, would be a concrete step in this regard.

As deepening inequalities and the continued downward pressure on wages of workers and reduction of work benefits are inconsistent with social harmony and can potentially lead to social conflicts, they would need to be addressed.

Political reforms and legal provisions for recognizing greater equality as regards race, gender and age are also essential to raising awareness and consciousness among businesses of these objectives. Protecting immigrants' workplace rights and civil rights should be embedded in immigration laws and enforcement of equal employment opportunity protections. In fact, the introduction of anti-discrimination laws is needed to ensure that employment growth and decent work do not disproportionately benefit the more privileged members of society.

Emerging challenges for policy interventions

Changes in the labour market brought on by increasing globalization have resulted in new policy challenges whose impact on inequality will require further studies.

Migrant and overseas employment, which has increased significantly in a globalized world, constitutes one such challenge. It is increasingly recognized that migrant workers come from families of relatively higher income in their home countries. With foreign remittances increasing, a direct income effect has been the increase in wage and income inequality in the sending country. In addition, as these workers are generally better educated and productive, their migration contributes to brain drain, disrupting the supply of important services including medical and health-care services and education, and resulting in higher prices or the reduction of social services for those left in the sending country. Careful consideration needs to be given to the potentially adverse effects of the growth of overseas employment and of foreign remittances on income distribution, particularly as developing countries encourage and promote overseas work as an important tool with which to address unemployment and foreign exchange deficits. These considerations need to be balanced against benefits such as higher incomes and gains in skills, productivity and work experience that are reaped upon the return of migrant workers.

Another emerging challenge is the growing rollback of enterprise non-wage benefits (for example, pension and health insurance). While this is perceived as helpful in generating employment and maintaining a competitive business environment, it has potential long-term implications. The competition among countries to attract businesses can lead to the establishment of a global standard that relies on the privatization and commercialization of benefit schemes. This privatization process in societies with poor consumer protection capabilities can potentially expose workers and their families to fraudulent business practices. In addition, under voluntary schemes, there may not be sufficient voluntary participation to create viable insurance programmes (whether privately or publicly operated). The efficiency benefits from the rollback in enterprise non-wage benefits should be balanced against the long-term overall impact on society and against their potential adverse long-term implications for health care and income security of workers as well as retirees.

Concluding remarks

Global economic inequalities have increased during the past two decades and income inequality within many countries has been rising since the 1980s. This chapter has shown that a high degree of inequality has a negative impact on subsequent economic outcomes and that better income and wealth redistribution can indeed promote sustainable economic growth that would generate a relative improvement in work opportunities. Though classical economic models suggest that wealth inequality is supportive of economic growth, based on the empirical evidence presented there is little doubt that reducing wealth inequality does not have a negative effect on economic growth. In fact, a high level of economic inequalities can retard economic growth by creating political demands for redistribution. Evidence suggests that economic growth and productivity are better supported by an equitable distribution of wealth and better healthcare and education. Also, the lack of access to credit for many in very unequal societies creates market inefficiencies. In these countries, increased equality would increase credit access and improve the efficiency of the economy, thereby raising the level of employment and work conditions for the poor.

Income inequality also hurts economic outcomes and, in turn, employment-generation through its impact on social inequalities such as those related to gender, health and education, among others. Where gender inequality is high, fewer resources are invested in human capital and ultimately in the future labour market. In addition, discrimination based on gender, ethnicity, age or other factors irrelevant to job performance introduces serious inefficiencies (not to mention injustices) into the labour market.

Good health is essential for a productive labour force, and low income is one of the major factors associated with poor health. The HIV/AIDS epidemic in Africa is one example of how population health can have seriously negative consequences for economic growth and employment generation, owing to the loss not only of human capital, but also of FDI.

Income inequality also affects the labour market by reinforcing educational disparities and breaking down social cohesion, hindering economic growth and employment-creation.

Finally, there are policies and strategies that Governments can pursue to promote and generate full employment and decent work, taking into account the issue of income inequality. Redistributive policies should be more widely implemented. Trade unions in their role of strengthening the position of workers in collective bargaining and promoting productivity growth represent another means of improving economic outcome by reducing inequality. Policies on employment and decent work should factor in political and legal reforms to ensure that such initiatives do not exacerbate inequalities in society and that they provide employment opportunities for all and protect the rights of workers.

The fact that deepening inequalities and declining wages and benefits reduce social cohesion and can lead to overt conflict should be confronted directly.

This chapter has also examined some emerging challenges for policy interventions owing to changes in the labour market resulting from increasing globalization. The impact on inequality of migrants and overseas employment, as well as of the increasing rollback of non-wage benefits such as pensions and health insurance, warrants further studies.

Notes

[1] It is important to consider that the behaviour of individual savings as income changes might be influenced by several factors, and it is therefore difficult to accept a priori the idea that marginal savings will increase with income.

Chapter V

Social protection, labour and work

In ensuring income security for workers, social protection plays an important role in the decent work for all agenda. A social protection system includes preventive and remedial schemes, informal networks and formal systems operated by Governments, local authorities, enterprises of employment and non-governmental organizations, ranging from religious institutions to single-issue charities and lobbying organizations.

Social security, as an important component of social protection, encompasses a narrower set of benefits and compensatory government schemes, such as social insurance and social assistance, dealing with compensation for illness, unemployment, maternity, disability and old age. In the developed countries of the world in the middle decades of the twentieth century, social security systems were the primary means of achieving social integration. They were also a means by which labour was made less dependent on, and less vulnerable to, market forces. The social security systems also had an efficiency function, facilitating employment with an objective of encouraging workers to acquire skills and to remain in the labour market so as to make use of them. In terms of the distribution of income between social groups, the welfare systems that emerged in developed countries were never very redistributive, in design or in effect.

In the post-1945 era, at the heart of the European social model which seemed to set the standard for emulation, was the central concept of social insurance. Within this scheme, contributions paid by employers or/and workers towards a collective fund, or funds, were matched by compensatory payments to workers adversely affected by contingency risks including involuntary unemployment, sickness, maternity, disability and old-age retirement. While there were universalistic elements (entitlements based solely on national citizenship), it was on the performance of labour or at least on the demonstrated willingness to perform labour that most income compensation schemes were largely based. In effect, they represented and supported industrial citizenship, that is to say, they were geared to a model of labour associated with industry, rather than with agriculture or services, a model in which full-time male employment was the overwhelming norm. It was thus what many observers have called a male bread-winner model that guided social protection policies. This type of social insurance system can work well only in a society with something close to full employment, in which contributions to insurance funds are roughly matched by the demands for benefits from them, and in which most of the demands for income transfers are short-term.

The labour-based schemes of State insurance were extended to developing countries while becoming steadily more extensive in scope and coverage in those industrialized countries where they had been the norm in the early post-1945 era. One result was that as benefits were extended, it was the men in stable full-time jobs and those closest to such forms of employment who benefited most, rather than those who were engaged in the most precarious and informal forms of labour and work.

In the era of globalization and social economic reform, social protection systems are under reconstruction across the world. Any strategy for promoting decent work must begin by considering the character of current systems of social support for work and training.

With liberalization, there has been a steady rollback in State systems of social security and a reduced expectation regarding the universality of State provision. Although these reversals have been observed almost everywhere, they have been strongest in some of the most developed "welfare state" countries, and evident as well in middle-income and developing countries, which were expected to be developing State-based social security systems.

Worldwide, there has been a shift to means-tested (targeted) schemes developed alongside a host of private savings-account schemes. Means-tested schemes target income transfers to those deemed to be in poverty, that is to say with an income less than some specified poverty level. Anybody who would fall into that situation would qualify for a benefit. Only a small percentage of the population would actually qualify at any one time, and only a percentage of that group would actually receive a benefit. Although few countries have come to rely almost entirely on means-testing, most countries have introduced a much greater degree of means-testing than used to be the case. This has happened for several reasons, including the fact that higher unemployment in the 1970s and 1980s put the contributory systems under fiscal pressure and the fact that more flexible labour markets and more informal working relationships meant that fewer people were covered by standard contributory schemes. Economic liberalization policies that ushered in commercialization of social policy also contributed to this trend. The main reason, however, seems to have been the desire of Governments to cut back on their public social spending.

Those pressures remain pervasive in developing countries where very few workers are in the types of employment that entitle them to standard social security transfers such as unemployment benefits or pensions. Yet, during the pre-globalization era, those countries had been expected to introduce or maintain such schemes. The result was that remarkably small percentages of the labour force came to have access to what were in fact rather privileged State benefits that merely reduced the economic vulnerability of relatively secure groups of workers, without reaching the most impoverished and the most economically insecure.

Meanwhile, in developed countries, from the 1970s onward as more people became dependent on intrinsically insecure labour markets, the overall need for State benefits increased; but it did so at a time when Governments everywhere were under pressure to cut public social spending as part of the macroeconomic strategy in the globalization era. Forms of social spending were depicted as unproductive, so that Governments were urged to shift to public investment that would facilitate private productive investment and to human capital spending. They were urged to shift to a greater degree towards active social policies, as opposed to passive policies, meaning those providing relatively unconditional benefits. Social benefits were seen as raising non-wage labour costs and as imposing a burden on employers, thereby impeding national competitiveness.

The claim that the systems of State social benefits have resulted in onerous non-wage labour costs, limiting job creation and eroding national competitiveness, has been influential, leading many Governments to introduce sharp cutbacks in social benefits and to shift more of the costs of providing social protection from the State and from enterprises onto workers and their informal private networks of support. In most parts of the world, for example, contribution rates have gone up for workers and have gone down for employers.

The result of the pursuit of competitiveness has been the introduction of a wave of cuts in public social protection, which should be characterized as representing not a race to the bottom, but rather a global trend of convergence towards a model of social protection in which private and privatized provision of a growing range of income transfers and services are expected to play a much greater, if not a dominant role (Alber and Standing, 2000). Where social spending has remained reasonably high, there has tended to be a shift from social protection per se to human capital expenditure.

In effect, the average composition of social income is being restructured, and with State benefits as a share of the total income of workers being cut almost everywhere, and with more and more workers being expected to rely on a privatized system and on their families or local communities. In most developing countries, statutory (mandatory) benefits have been receding even before they reached more than a very small proportion of the population.

Several principles have had powerful effects on the global trends in social protection systems, although none of them have been very successfully implemented. The first is that there should be greater targeting of the needy and poor, on the grounds that there exist limited and shrinking public resources for social protection and that this is the most efficient way to achieve poverty alleviation. The second is that social protection needs to counter social exclusion and thus must induce those who for whatever reason, have been marginalized, to return to the mainstream of society through employment. The third principle is that private provision of benefits is more efficient and sustainable than State provision, which was long presumed to be the only means to provide universal and equitable social protection. Although some observers still maintain that State provision is essential, the strong trend in the globalization era, where market forces have been encouraged, has been towards the privatization and commercialization of social policy.

While there have been some counter-examples in a few countries that may be considered, it is the main tendencies in each of the main areas of social protection that are described briefly below. This will give us a picture of the emerging social underpinning of globalizing labour markets and thus a more complete understanding of the social context of emerging patterns of employment and work.

Health care: costs, access and "employability"

Health-care systems are experiencing strain in most countries, owing to demographic trends including ageing, rising costs of health care and the onslaught of communicable diseases such as HIV/AIDS, malaria and tuberculosis. The strain has also been linked to a shift in the emphasis of political rhetoric, from collective social solidarity to individual responsibility.

Worldwide, public provision based on universal entitlement and free or highly subsidized access has been on the retreat. Around the world, most people are dissatisfied with the health-care system in their country, and this is the case even in the richest countries (see, for example, Donelan and others, 1999). The crucial point of relevance to the effort to ensure decent work and employment is that a rising proportion of workers are not covered by protective measures in case of ill health, and more face rising costs. Almost everywhere, an accident or a long spell of serious ill health is likely to leave a person in financial difficulties.

In most developing countries, the absence of a functioning public-health system has long been a primary cause of social and economic insecurity (although the vast majority of workers and their families in developing countries do face much worse crises). Indeed, according to the World Health Organization (WHO) and some other observers, the situation of workers in low-income developing countries, which has deteriorated relative to that of workers in developed countries, has not been helped by enforced cutbacks in public social spending under the aegis of structural adjustment programmes.

Even in developed countries, the system is under strain. Increasingly, there is a reluctance to see health care as a collective responsibility, in which the more fortunate cross-subsidize the less fortunate.

A new trend in the United States of America is towards individualized health-savings accounts (HSAs), which, introduced in 2003, allow workers with high-deductible health insurance plans to set aside part of their wages, tax-free, to pay for their medical expenses. This move shifts the costs onto the workers and has tended to erode employer-sponsored health plans even further. This represents part of the financialization of enterprise benefits, and a group of major banks have established an HSA Council to assist in the spread of health-savings accounts.

This phenomenon deserves to be highlighted because it represents part of the global trend towards privatization. Financialization arises from a shift from direct provision to private, personal financial responsibility. One danger is that the relatively insurable, that is to say, healthy and young educated workers, would benefit relative to others like the sick and disabled, those on low incomes, and the elderly, who will end up paying higher premiums (precisely because they have a higher probability of illness) which lower their social incomes. As a result, income inequality would increase more than might have been the case if only earned incomes had been assessed. Many more may be unable or unwilling to pay those premiums and may thus lose protection altogether.

Another trend is for companies to transfer costs onto their workers by shifting to health insurance with high deductibles, in other words, to offer workers moderate premiums for health- care coverage, while obliging them to pay a high initial amount should they incur health-related expenses. This reform risks being inegalitarian in as much as those less likely to be ill, namely young and better-educated higher earners, will end up paying less. This is one way in which firms have been saving money, but at the cost of effective social protection.

The problems being faced in developed countries are still modest compared with the acute crisis in developing countries. Access to public health care in these countries has often been rudimentary and largely restricted to favoured urban industrial areas; for this and other reasons, people have had to rely more on private services, for which they had to pay. Cuts in social spending have tended to restrict growth in public provision, while health-care needs are rising.

Besides experiencing lack of access to affordable general medical care, many workers in developing countries work in dangerous and unsafe conditions, and surveys have shown that they are aware of this and fear the consequences (see box V1). Those performing agricultural labour are among the worst affected (International Labour Organization, 2003c).

Workers in countries in transition from State socialism to a market economy have also been severely affected by such conditions. In these countries, the dismantling of the former State-operated health-care systems has rarely been matched by the establishment of effective new systems. As a result, though, many millions of workers are at risk, the public-health systems in their countries are not capable of helping those who become ill or injured.

Globally, the drive to expand production, to accelerate economic growth and to maintain or improve cost competitiveness has led to a disregard for basic preventive measures. This, in turn, has contributed to lackadaisical labour inspection and led to the closure or erosion of health and safety departments in enterprises, as firms cut costs and downsized, decentralized or normalized their employment structures.

An important factor is the trend away from statutory regulation to self-regulation as part of the liberalization that has accompanied globalization. Self-regulation may endanger greater work insecurity. To appreciate this, one must comprehend the rationale for self-regulation as a result of liberalization, whereby policymakers have been encouraged to curb reliance on complex safety codes, cut back "generous" compensation for work-related ill health and cut health programmes for workers.

The argument is, partly, that high health costs make firms less competitive with firms in other countries that do not have to bear such costs and eventually drive employers to informalize their labour. Second, it is claimed that complex regulations make workers and employers more careless and that imposing the costs on employers would introduce the factor of moral hazard as regards workers: not having to bear those costs, they would become more reckless. Third, it is claimed that, if employers have to pay the costs when workers are injured or fall ill, they will turn to indirect forms of labour through casualization and outsourcing.

These arguments are controversial. Old-style statutory regulation of working conditions may indeed be paternalistic; but the self-regulation model encourages opportunism on the part of some employers and induces cost-cutting that puts many workers at risk of impoverishment through an accident or ill health. It must be appreciated that workers rarely know the health hazards or

---

Box V.1
The missing statistics on work insecurity

Workplace accidents are chronically underreported, and the illnesses associated with labour or employment are hard to monitor even in well-regulated labour markets, in part because many of them emerge some time after the events that caused them. Employers are, understandably, reluctant to link incidents of ill health or accidents to their workplace or procedures and prefer to attribute responsibility to the workers or to social factors outside the workplace

Fearing the costs of health care, they may distance themselves from responsibility by making workers accept a "self-employment" or "contract work" status, they may oblige them to take out private health insurance as a condition of employment, or they may use short-term employment contracts so that if a worker becomes prone to illness or is injured, employment termination will be relatively inexpensive.

Through these various means, the linkages between workplaces and work insecurity can be hidden.

the probabilities of ill health, and that in the absence of such knowledge, they are likely to opt for an income that assures them current consumption, rather than pay an insurance premium for possible income at some future date.

Without formal regulations and institutional mechanisms to prohibit the requirement to work long hours and to prevent exposure to dangerous working conditions, hard-pressed workers may take excessive risks — or find they cannot refuse to do so — because they have family members in need, perhaps because of illness, or schooling costs to cover (International Labour Organization, 2004a). Risks and hazards result in adverse outcomes for some workers. If they are in that vulnerable near-poor category, the result could be impoverishment and an inability to cope, leading to longer-term illness, loss of productivity or demoralization resulting in labour-force detachment within a cycle of despair.

Disability benefits

An important form of social protection comprises benefits for those experiencing one or more forms of disability, be it physical or mental. Several million people are in this situation, but many of them have little or no hope of State support, although disability or incapacity benefits have been integral to the social schemes of welfare States from their inception.

Two issues are crucial. First, do disability benefits reach those in need of help, and do they take the form that is most appropriate? Second, do disability benefits help those with disabilities play a full and productive role in society or do such benefits hinder them?

In regard to the first question, there has been considerable concern that the criteria used to determine eligibility are often complex and stigmatizing, resulting in a situation where many persons with disabilities do not apply for benefits or where many apply without success.

In regard to the second question, a primary concern has been that disability benefits could push people into both a poverty trap and a disability trap. If a person receives an income transfer because he or she is deemed disabled, that person will have less of an incentive to rectify the situation or prove that he or she can do some work. So goes the conventional argument.

In part because of ageing, the number of people receiving disability benefits in developed countries has risen very substantially in recent years. This has caused policymakers to review State policy and, in some countries, has resulted in reforms that have tightened eligibility in order to encourage or induce many persons with disabilities to enter the labour market and take jobs. In the process, there has been a sharpening of the always-subjective distinction between "abled" and "disabled".

The introduction of activity requirements has put an increased burden on the person with impairments to prove eligibility, which affects the propensity to claim. This may drive persons with disabilities into the open labour market, and more of them into unemployment. And it may discourage some of them from being economically active. What is clear is that workers with disabilities tend to be heavily disadvantaged in the labour market. The best way to ease their difficulties is to ensure that employers provide reasonable accommodation so as to make it possible for such workers to overcome their impediments in the workplace. A rights-based approach, as embedded in the Convention on the Rights of Persons with Disabilities (United Nations, 2006g),[1] is a good move in that direction. In article 27 of the Convention:

> States Parties recognize the right of persons with disabilities to work, on an equal basis with others; this includes the right to the opportunity to gain a living by work freely chosen or accepted in a labour market and work environment that is open, inclusive and accessible to persons with disabilities. States Parties shall safeguard and promote the realization of the right to work, including for those who acquire a disability during the course of employment.

This should be the guiding principle observed by all State parties.

Pension reforms: are pensions dying?

Pension systems around the world have been in a state of turmoil with the advent of globalization, with numerous Governments trying out a wide variety of reforms and resorting to the establishment of numerous commissions or special inquiries in order to find an answer to the fiscal and labour-market challenges.

At the heart of the problem is global ageing, with the rising old-age dependency ratio making it difficult to develop or to sustain the classic State and enterprise-based defined-benefit pensions, which was the hallmark of welfare States throughout the twentieth century (United Nations, 2007). Companies around the world are rapidly phasing out such schemes, while Governments are cutting back on public commitments.

The new and popular approach to easing the burden of population ageing on the pension systems is to try to encourage more workers in their fifties and sixties — and even seventies — to stay in the labour force or to return to it. This represents a reversal of a trend started in the 1970s and 1980s when many Governments in developed countries responded to rising unemployment by introducing early retirement schemes, through which to ease older employees out of the labour force.

It is almost certain that one aspect of old-style defined-benefit schemes, namely the practice of linking pension levels to final salaries, adversely affected the employment of older workers. This means that older workers in such schemes are penalized if they take pay cuts, or slide into lower-level jobs in their pre-retirement years. In ageing societies, this makes no sense, since it discourages older workers from staying in the labour force, and also encourages firms to push out relatively expensive older workers. In the interest of enabling older workers to remain economically active if they so wish, the linkage of pensions to final salaries should be phased out.

Although it is mostly in developed parts of the world that, a "greying" working population has been linked to an impending pension crisis, the phenomenon has affected some developing countries as well. For example, China had 36 million old-age pensioners by 2000 and the old-age dependency ratio was rising continuously (Zheng, 2002). By then, pensioners from large and medium-sized State-owned enterprises constituted 37 per cent of their workforces, and various estimates suggest that on current trends, pensions will have risen from 7 per cent of the total wage bill in 1998 to 40 per cent by 2030 (Feng, 2001). The hitherto relatively high pension, which was nearly 90 per cent of average earnings in 1990, has begun to fall.

A crisis of non-entitlement to pensions is looming in China. Contribution rates have started to rise and the number of years of contributions required to gain entitlement to a pension has gone up. This is a familiar story elsewhere in the world; but with rural-urban and urban-urban migrants making up a rapidly growing proportion of the labour force, it is almost certain that a rising proportion of workers are being shut out of enterprise-based pension entitlement altogether. Many enterprises simply do not enrol migrant workers in social insurance, thereby avoiding contribution to a sizeable wedge in the wage bill (over 30 per cent).

In developed countries, where State pension systems became well-entrenched, the pattern of the changes that are taking place is clear, even if it varies a little from country to country. The average age of statutory pensionable retirement is rising. In European countries, over the past decade or so, it has risen by about half a year for men on average and by about one year for women. It is still lower on average for women, even though women tend to live longer and thus have more years of paid retirement than men. However, this tells only part of the story, since women still have a much lower probability of gaining entitlement to a decent pension or to any pension at all.

Unequal access to pensions is certainly not a feature just of developed countries. Surveys of the ILO (2004a) have found similarly unequal entitlement patterns within formal enterprises in various other countries. Differential entitlement to pensions is a very important source of income inequality among workers all over the world.

Indeed, in most developing countries, pensions have reached only a minority of workers, although Latin America has had a long tradition of social security schemes. Basically, leading Latin American countries have been moving towards a multi-pillar system, in which the mix of a basic pension with social insurance and individualized savings-account schemes has been encouraged. On the other hand, in much of Asia, only small minorities have had access to any sort of pension.

Worldwide, the average number of years of contributions required to obtain a State pension has been going up and the number of years of contributions required for entitlement to a full State pension has been going up even more (International Labour Organization, 2004a). There has been a virtual collapse of company-based defined-benefit pensions and a sharp shift towards defined-contribution schemes, with a decline in the share of workers in any company scheme. Public sector pensions, long a major source of privilege for civil servants, have tended to fall into line with other pensions.

Very significantly, contribution rates have tended to rise, but the rates for workers have risen more than for employers, thereby subtly altering the structure of social income. In a number of countries, including some developing countries in the 1990s, the average contribution rate for workers has risen to a level much higher than that for employers, which is contrary to the provisions of article 71 of International Labour Convention No. 102, concerning Minimum Standards of Social Security, 1952.

Finally, some countries have been trying to make their pension systems more flexible by linking pension levels or contribution rates to changes in life expectancy, so as to correct for the fact that past actuarial predictions had underestimated the increase in longevity and were therefore inaccurate.

Many major corporations are not only abandoning their defined-benefit pensions but capping health-care spending for their retired workers. In short, the economic security long associated with formal employment is withering away.

It has to be recognized that company-based defined-benefit pension schemes are anachronistic in a world economy in which average employment tenure is five or six years, even in developed countries. That system was developed on the basis of a presumed model of "lifetime" employment, with very few years of post-employment retirement, and at a time when average life expectancy for workers was actually less than the statutory retirement age.

In this era of labour flexibility, companies rarely expect, or even want, most of their workers to stay in their jobs for 25 years or more. Paternalistic employers and "loyal" workers are scarcely the norm for flexible labour markets, and companies are adjusting their benefits to behavioural expectations. Companies could assist workers in saving or improving their lifetime income security, but that may not be through twentieth century defined-benefit schemes based on the level of earnings received in the few years prior to retirement.

The future of pension systems is uncertain, but there should be a move towards increased flexibility, with more variability in the age of statutory retirement, so as to allow people to choose when to retire, and to retire with higher pensions if they do so later. This is already happening in some countries, such as Canada, where the State pension can be taken at any time between the ages of 60 and 70. Meanwhile, the trend towards earlier retirement, so notable in the 1970s and 1980s, has come to a halt, and with rising life expectancy and healthier later lives, may even go into reverse. That would be a historic reversal, with implications for pensions and for work that have yet to be adequately considered.

Unemployment insurance benefits

Traditionally, most workers had little protection against the risk of unemployment. However, during the twentieth century, two forms of protection spread: severance pay and unemployment insurance benefits. Severance pay has been a privilege of a minority of the employed across the world. By contrast, unemployment insurance was always regarded as a central pillar of welfare States, shielding workers from the worst effects of unemployment and also acting, with the onset of a recession, as a macroeconomic stabilizer by maintaining consumption so that aggregate demand would not fall by much.

Unfortunately, labour-market liberalization has been associated with the erosion of unemployment benefit systems as the number of unemployed in the world is apparently rising. In most countries, those becoming unemployed or remaining unemployed for any length of time are experiencing a higher level of economic insecurity than was the case with the onset of globalization.

As of 2007, only a minority of the unemployed in most of the developed countries are entitled to, and are receiving, unemployment insurance benefits — about a third in the United States, about 40 per cent in many of the European Union countries and a smaller proportion elsewhere. Moreover, the proportion receiving those benefits has been declining. One reason for the decline is that more workers are in labour statuses that do not entitle them to receive such benefits. Another is that more of the unemployed are in long-term unemployment, while Governments are tightening the conditions for and shortening the duration of such entitlement. A high proportion of the unemployed are young labour-force entrants and immigrants, who have not built up sufficiently long employment records to be eligible for benefits.

Two factors have contributed to the tightening of conditions for entitlement. Policymakers, set on reducing public spending, have seen the cutting of unemployment benefits as a relatively simple matter, since the unemployed are an easy target and unemployment has been much higher than when unemployment insurance benefits were at their peak in the 1950s and 1960s. Nowadays, the unemployed in developed countries are more likely to be depicted as "lazy" and "living off the dole" as public dissatisfaction with old-style welfare States has risen in most, if not all, countries. The average voter feels detached from their plight. Cutting unemployment benefits and cutting the duration of entitlement have been politically popular moves, or at least have been less unpopular than cutting benefits in other areas of social protection.

Even countries that have long provided adequate and long-lasting coverage have moved in the direction of cutting, or restricting access to, unemployment benefits. A recent example is Sweden, where in October 2006 the Government announced cuts in benefits as part of its initial programme, even stating that this was to facilitate income tax cuts for the better off. Moreover, the Government has said that it intends to require workers to pay more into unemployment benefit funds directed by the trade unions. It is likely that this will induce more low-earning workers to opt out of the unions and the funds. This could spell a difficult period for unionization in Sweden, which might encourage other countries to follow suit.

In the United States, unemployment insurance benefits, introduced in 1935, have always been short-duration transfers, although Congress can vote for a temporary increase in the time period over which they can be received during a recession. Paying for up to six months may have seemed reasonable enough when a large proportion of the unemployed were temporarily laid off, waiting for a recall to their jobs, as was formerly the case; but with more flexible labour relations, with the increased concern with being "competitive" and with many more structural job losses, the proportion of layoffs has gone down sharply (Groshen and Potter, 2003). As a result, more of the unemployed experience longer spells of unemployment and thus loss of access to unemployment benefits.

In continental Europe, Governments have been urged to curb the activity of their unemployment benefit systems in an effort to lower stubbornly high unemployment and many have done so. The results, however, have been mixed. In Germany, the Hartz IV reforms, which had been intended to cut unemployment, ran into immediate problems because they put an estimated 1 million workers in a position where they received benefits of a greater value than the incomes they would have earned in the jobs they had been expected to accept.

Another factor contributing to the tightening of entitlement conditions has been the tendency of unemployed workers to stay unemployed, rather than take jobs that would pay them less. Policymakers used this to justify cutting benefit levels, but such an approach was found to be incapable of inducing the unemployed to accept low-paid jobs, especially when many of those jobs were part-time, casual or unpromising in other respects.

As a result, Governments have resorted more and more to behavioural con-ditionality for determining entitlement to benefits, effectively trying thereby to coerce the unemployed into jobs. They have, inter alia, tightened job-seeking requirements and obliged the unemployed both to accept jobs not necessarily within the range of those corresponding to their skills and work experience and to be prepared to change location in search of employment.

Besides the Republic of Korea, there are few developing countries that have any kind of functional unemployment benefit systems. In most of those that do have some sort of scheme, only tiny minorities of the unemployed are entitled to participate in them. It is not much of an exaggeration to say that the prospects for comprehensive State-based unemployment protection in the global economy are very dim indeed.

In sum, globally, the reality is that a growing proportion of the unemployed either have no access to unemployment benefits of any kind or have to demon-strate that they are "deserving" of unemployment assistance, which increasingly is being given to them as a discretionary allowance contingent on the fulfilment of specified behavioural obligations. In such circumstances, entitlement to an unem-ployment benefit ceases to be a social right. So far, Governments have resisted the temptation to privatize unemployment insurance, but some economists have pro-posed this option (for example, Orszag and Snower, 2002). The danger is that this would not help the most insecure and disadvantaged, as the costs might be pro-hibitive for them owing to their high-risk status and low income.

Family and childcare benefits and care work compensation

In most countries, family benefits were among the last to spread as welfare States developed. These have been effective in reducing the incidence of poverty among children, which is critical for their satisfactory development and learning. Con-siderable applied research exists also to show that there is a negative impact on child development when mothers are obliged to work full-time in the first few months of the child's life (Brooks-Gunn, Han and Waldfogel, 2002; Waldfogel, Han and Brooks-Gunn, 2002).

There is also evidence of the positive role of organized group care during pre-school age of 2 or 3, in preparing children for both social and academic success in school (Sylva, 2004). These pieces of evidence show that the work of childcare has considerable benefit in terms of externalities for children and society.

In light of the value of childcare and other forms of work that are often unpaid, Governments are being drawn to consider more ingenious ways of providing income security for those doing non-income earning work (see, for example., Daly, 2001; Lethbridge, 2006). The most popular proposal has been to provide regular "wage" payments to those doing care work, whether they are caring for their own children, elderly, frail parents, or for others who are not close kin.

The standard example of this type of policy is maternity leave, whereby a new mother is provided with a financial payment for a few months (or, in a few cases, up to two years) after the birth of a child. In recent years, some countries have extended this to include provision of paternity leave, or have provided new parents with the option of sharing a period of paid leave between them.

A more novel approach entails the payment of allowances to enable someone to focus on the care of children, relatives or even neighbours, often for a long period or even quasi-permanently. Among policies moving in that direction are childcare tax credits, as developed in Germany. The arguments in favour of such schemes are that they are universal, being given to all parents, and, potentially at least, non-labourist in design (that is to say they do not, require the prior performance of labour as a condition for entitlement), thereby providing support for all, regardless of whether or not they were previously in employment, and thus allowing coverage for those doing other forms of work. The criticisms are that they are very costly, tend to result in a fall in the female labour supply and are hard to legitimize among voters.

From social insurance to social assistance

It is time to take stock of the effect of the trends in social security on decent work and employment. The principle of social insurance has always been the cornerstone of social security systems. However, it is automatically weak in economies dominated by informal economic activities and it is surely being weakened further by the growth of more flexible labour relations. In such circumstances, it is unrealistic to envisage social security as the cornerstone of social protection in the future, given the growing informalization, labour casualization, offshoring and labour-market flexibility through which the economic liberalization that defines globalization is being pursued.

In developing countries, but also increasingly in developed ones where flexible and precarious forms of labour are spreading, only a small or declining proportion of workers are covered by social insurance. It also tends to be regressive in societies dominated by informal labour markets, since it benefits privileged minorities who are employed in the formal sector, rather than all those struggling to create meaningful livelihoods. Careful studies have shown that social insurance not only fails to reach the majority, but does not reach those most in need in developing countries (see, for example, Justino, 2005; and Evans and others, 2006, for a case study of Viet Nam).

If the employer's costs of complying are high, firms can take steps fairly easily to avoid making the contributions, primarily by informalizing their labour relations. That has led some Governments to shift the burden of contributions from employers to workers, which has led the latter to wonder whether it would not in fact be preferable to take the money in wages, rather than contribute to what is, at best, a forced savings scheme, from which they may or may not receive some return at some unknown time in the future. The result has been a predictable lack of interest in participating and consequently a loss of entitlement.

The other pillar of traditional social security systems in the twentieth century was social assistance, which aims to help people living in poverty secure a minimal standard of living and, ultimately, to enable them escape poverty. The argument is that the State should target its limited funds to relieving poverty, and to do this, it must identify the most poor by testing for their means of support, or, in effect, their income, financial savings and financially valuable assets. In the 1980s and 1990s, many countries, including most developed ones, extended their use of means-testing. They also added more behavioural testing to their armory of conditionalities. In other words, to gain entitlement, recipients were required to undertake work-related activities or demonstrate that they had lost their jobs involuntarily. A growing number of developing countries have moved in the same direction.

The arguments in favour of means-testing in social assistance in general claim, first, that it targets the poor and most needy; second, that it achieves legitimacy with voters; and, third, that it ensures the best use of limited public resources.

The criticisms are both theoretical and empirical. First, evidence shows conclusively that means-tested schemes have a low take-up rate. In other words, only a small proportion of the eligible people gain access to the benefits. This has been found to be the case in advanced welfare States such as

Sweden and Germany as well as in developing countries where the required administrative infrastructure and capacity may be lacking. There are many reasons for such an outcome. The poor and vulnerable tend to be unaware of the existence of such schemes, or unsure of whether they might qualify. They may fear the judgement of discovering that they are not abiding by the law in some way, or believe that the nature of their activity would disqualify them for benefits or think that their income is above the "poverty line" stipulated for entitlement, when in fact it is not.

Second, means-tested schemes are often flawed through their reliance on a poverty line, particularly as applied in developing countries characterized by extensive labour informality, seasonality and income insecurity. If the line is established as a specific income received over a specific short reference period, it becomes very hard to determine eligibility over any lengthy period, given the likelihood of income fluctuations.

A third criticism of means-tested social assistance schemes is that they tend to have a perverse distributional outcome, often not benefiting the poorest, but assisting the near-poor, who have greater knowledge of the social security system and less fear of its administrative requirements. Thus, means-testing risks giving to those who are not in need, and not giving to those who are in need.

Fourth, means-testing creates severe poverty traps, assets traps and unemployment traps. These traps arise from the fact that if a person receives a benefit only if his income is below a certain amount, at some point he will lose the benefit if he earns more. However, it is possible that the extra earning is less than the lost benefit, meaning that he is likely to be worse off as a result of earning more. If a person with any meaningful savings is disqualified for benefits such as food stamps and those provided by public health-care programmes for the poor and disabled, there will be an incentive for him or her to run down savings. This poverty trap creates a strong disincentive to save.

All forms of such traps create powerful moral hazards. A moral hazard arises if a person continues to rely on the benefit rather than take a job that is available, simply because he or she would be worse off or scarcely any better off as a result of accepting employment. Alternatively, an individual may not declare the employment for fear of being penalized through loss of the benefit, rationalizing the decision based on the fact that, in his or her particular case, the employment may pay less than the benefit.

Fifth, social assistance schemes typically impose a stigma on recipients and potential recipients. People do not like to beg or to rely on help that they perceive to be a sign of their own failure, or to be seen as exposing their plight through applying for benefits and thereby demonstrating their inadequacy for coping economically by themselves.

Finally, not only does the application of means tests involve high administrative costs, but ultimately their application is discretionary, with local bureaucrats having enough autonomy to be able to decide who receives benefits and who is denied them.

In sum, while traditional social insurance seems to be losing relevance as the cornerstone of social protection in the era of globalization and increasing labour-market flexibility, social assistance is also facing challenges. One of the challenges is a political one rooted in the public frustration over the perceived ineffectiveness of such programmes in helping people get off welfare. However, attempts to target the needy through means-testing and to introduce, through behavioural testing, incentives that encourage those receiving assistance to improve their situation, have created their own problems.

The spread of individualized savings accounts

In various areas of social protection, Governments are encouraging the spread of individualized savings accounts that are either mandatory or subsidized by means of tax incentives, notably in the areas of pensions and health care, but also in areas such as unemployment insurance. The debates centred around this trend have been highly charged and inconclusive.

On the positive side, as those individualized accounts that allow for individual choice are self-funding, they enable Governments to cut public social spending and help them spread "popular capitalism". They are also depicted by advocates as replacing non-affordable pay-as-you-go defined-benefit schemes. Above all, individualized accounts are presented as giving individuals greater financial control over perceived risks.

The counter-arguments are considerable. Critics have presented evidence to show that such accounts are regressive and very costly to administer and usually depend on government subsidies for their development and survival. Critics also point out that the individualization of social security undermines the critical element of social insurance, namely, the promotion of social solidarity, whereby the more fortunate effectively subsidize the less fortunate. With individualized accounts, those who cannot afford to contribute to individualized savings, and those not in jobs enabling them to do so, are put at a big disadvantage, risking being left with no protection.

Finally, critics have worried that the privatized individualized savings schemes have given enormous financial power to a small number of major multinational "pension fund managers" and their equivalents in the sphere of health care insurance and other social services, which are outside easy regulation at the national level.

There is an evolving debate on the potential role of individualized savings accounts in employment insurance, as opposed to unemployment insurance. One proposal is to establish "temporary earnings replacement accounts" (Kling, 2006). All workers would be given such an account and encouraged to deposit part of their income in that account, from which they could make withdrawals at their discretion should they lose their jobs, up to an amount set by the government. Workers could even borrow from the account, replenishing it out of future earnings. There are obvious dangers inherent in such a scheme. Once again, the usual response to a crisis in the traditional social security instrument is to envisage an individualistic, non-solidaristic replacement scheme. Such proposals look as if they would benefit the relatively successful among the unemployed, that is to say, those who could earn enough to repay the borrowings.

While individualized savings accounts in all forms of social protection do not benefit the most insecure and poorest groups, they are nevertheless almost certain to figure increasingly in twenty-first century systems of social protection. Governments and their policy advisers should try to ensure that those accounts do so within a context of adequate economic security for those who cannot benefit from social protection schemes.

The fiscalization of social security

While the drift towards means-testing and individualized accounts has been growing, the social security systems of developed countries have, rather quietly, been transformed by a growing reliance on fiscal policy as a means of providing social security. To put it bluntly, while many more jobs in developed countries are paying low wages and providing fewer benefits, Governments have been trying to use fiscal policy to reduce employers' non-wage labour costs.

Labour subsidies to employers have proliferated. A large aspect of fiscalization of social policy has been the spread of labour-related tax credits.

Such schemes have been adopted in many developed countries, particularly the United States and those in Western Europe. Although the tax credit goes to many workers in services such as catering and retail trade, it also subsidizes workers in tradable sectors such as garments and textiles. As such, it raises important questions about market distortion and trade subsidies, since it reduces the direct labour costs of enterprises competing against potential imports. This may become an issue in future World Trade Organization rounds of trade liberalization negotiations.

There are other potential drawbacks with tax credits, since they are essentially labour subsidies. Subsidies are by definition selective, and they also constitute a method of lowering costs. By lowering the cost of labour, they reduce the pressure on employers to allocate labour efficiently. They are more likely to favour labour-intensive technologies, but that may well be at the cost of longer-term dynamic efficiency.

Concluding remarks

Social protection should be an integral part of society and an integral part of decent work and employment. In sickness and in health, in employment and in unemployment, all people need social protection and basic economic security.

Although some observers have claimed that excessive social spending impedes economic growth, in that it crowds out private spending and investment, there is no statistical correlation to support that claim, at least not below about one third of gross domestic product (GDP), which is well above what most countries spend. Indeed, there is strong evidence that social spending assists growth when it increases from a very low level to about one quarter of GDP, since the social spending can boost aggregate demand, improve productivity and facilitate the emergence of a stable, committed labour force in productive employment.

Others have observed that countries that did spend a high share of GDP on social schemes have done best with globalization. It may be that countries that had already established strong welfare systems before globalization had in place mechanisms enabling them to survive better in the face of more open economies and the increased pressure to be internationally competitive. Yet even then, they have been forced to cut back on social security provision and entitlements as cost pressures have threatened to erode that competitiveness. Regardless, the fact remains that decent work requires a decent social protection system.

There are a range of services and benefits that could facilitate decent work. For example, the family has always provided the first form of social protection, but was expected to decline as the main provider in modern welfare States. As families are becoming more fragile and temporary, there are a greater number of negotiations on what conditions are to be applied in the provision of support. Meanwhile, with modernization, the State was expected to take over many of the protective functions of the family and neighbourhood. That has changed. Now the predominant position is that the market should prevail and commercial services and private insurance benefits should take up much of the slack being left by the retreat of social insurance. It is far from clear that this can be achieved. Gradually, a consensus seems to be emerging that, at the very least, the State should provide a universal floor of social protection, upon which social insurance, private insurance and other schemes can be built.

Two concerns have emerged within the context of the ongoing restructuring of social security. One is that a country's social protection system should actively promote economic growth, competitiveness and employment. In this regard, there is a popular phrase that has gained ground inside the Commission of the European Union, and more recently in ILO, namely, "social protection as a productive factor", encapsulating the view that social protection reforms should be geared towards the promotion of employment and evaluated according to that criterion. The challenge is to ensure that social and economic rights are not sacrificed to the interests of short-term allocative efficiency and the pursuit of cost-cutting to boost competitiveness. If priority is given to schemes that seem to offer the prospect of promoting labour productivity and "competitiveness", there may be a tendency to downgrade policies and schemes that protect the most insecure and impoverished in society.

The second concern, which is more worrisome for those concerned with social equity and decent work, relates to the increasing exertion of pressure on the poor, the economically insecure and the otherwise disadvantaged to behave in ways that the State determines to be socially desirable. Sometimes this is carried out using the language of reciprocity, according to which the poor must be prepared to meet certain work obligations if they are to be deemed deserving of benefits. However, this chapter has shown that social assistance schemes set up along these lines, albeit much favoured by reformers over the past two decades, have generated extensive poverty traps and unemployment traps.

The challenge that social protection systems face in the twenty-first century is a serious one. There is a dire need for creative and responsible approaches to promoting the agenda of decent work for all in a changing world.

Notes

[1] Adopted by the General Assembly on 13 December 2006 at United Nations Headquarters in New York. It had 100 Signatories as of 11 July 2007.

Chapter VI

Demand-side employment schemes

In most countries, Governments are expected to assist the unemployed (International Labour Organization, 2004a) through the provision of income security. It is less clear, though, what types of interventions are most likely to benefit individuals and their communities.

In both developed and developing countries, Governments have promoted employment directly through various special measures designed to create demand for labour, although they have given less attention or fewer resources to measures designed to promote decent work. The present chapter reviews the most popular policies promoting jobs and employment, such as public works, food-for-work schemes, workfare and labour subsidies, examining their impact on decent work.

This chapter also seeks to bring out the social implications of such special measures, including their distributional aspects and the tendency for all of them to involve large "deadweight", "displacement" and "substitution" effects.

In analysing special demand-side measures, it must always be remembered that they inevitably involve spending public resources that have an opportunity cost, in that the money allocated could have been spent on other schemes, some of which might have larger or more sustained effects on employment and work. This consideration emphasizes the fact that it is extremely difficult to evaluate

---

Box VI.1
What do Chinese workers want government to do for the unemployed?

In a 2001 International Labour Organization survey on what government should do for individuals who become unemployed, Chinese workers were asked if they agreed or disagreed with a selection of policy responses. Only 3.6 per cent agreed that government should do nothing; 86 per cent agreed that it should provide unemployment benefits; 82.5 per cent agreed that — Government should provide public works for the unemployed; 88.9 per cent agreed that there should be training schemes for them; and 85.8 per cent agreed that Government should help them relocate in their search for alternative employment.

the effectiveness of such special measures, in part because of the difficulty of identifying or measuring the *externalities* and the longer-term effects.

Employment subsidies

Employment subsidies, whereby employers are offered financial support for the extra jobs they create, account for a large percentage of expenditure on active labour-market programmes in many countries members of the Organization for Economic Cooperation and Development (OECD). The advocates of low-wage employment subsidies argue that such subsidies help relatively unskilled workers obtain low-paid jobs, which they would otherwise be unable to obtain, since their potential productivity is below the market wage. It has been stated that low-wage subsidies are both non-discriminatory and cost-effective. They enable employers to hire more workers, contributing to the fall in unemployment, which in turn causes most of the subsidy to be paid out as direct or indirect labour compensation.

Most employment subsidies are aimed at specific target groups, such as low-wage, less skilled workers, the long-term unemployed, youth, older persons and persons with disabilities. By targeting the more vulnerable groups, they counteract social exclusion. They also contribute to the reduction of long-term unemployment and in the long run tend to pay for themselves.

Among the biggest subsidies are earned-income tax credits, usually a refundable income tax credit for low-income working individuals or families. They encourage and reward employment, boosting labour-force participation among less skilled workers, and may be effective in fighting poverty.

Critics of employment subsidies emphasize that they tend to twist the demand for labour towards less skilled, lower-paid employment, thus encouraging labour-intensive production, resulting in lower productivity. Such subsidies are also likely to encourage inefficient allocation of labour and distort relative prices, and are likely to be a subsidy to capital, rather than to workers, allowing firms to pay lower wages, knowing that the incomes of workers are being topped up by the subsidy.

Moreover, employment subsidies tend to discriminate against older, well-established firms in favour of new, growing firms. This is intrinsically inequitable, since it penalizes firms that have been providing employment for some time and this could result in a substitution of subsidized jobs in new firms for non-subsidized jobs in older firms. The net effect on jobs could thus be very limited.

In the global context, many subsidies, especially those intended to boost certain sectors and, often, help export industries or strengthen sectors threatened by imports, are likely to become an issue before the World Trade Organization in that they may be construed as constituting an unfair trade practice. They may not be deliberately selective of export or import sectors but there can be little doubt that, at the margin, they influence national competitiveness.

Labour subsidies tend to go to the less poor, rather than to the most insecure. The reason is that they support those actually in employment (Marx, 2005).

Social funds

Social funds have been promoted as effective means of generating employment and economic activity in developing countries. They have been developed by the World Bank in the late 1980s, at a time when the Washington Consensus and structural adjustment programmes were being criticized for having generated a rise in poverty and more labour displacement than labour reabsorption. The first such fund was launched in Bolivia in 1987. Since then, they have been introduced in almost all Latin American and Caribbean countries and in about half of all sub-Saharan African countries. The World Bank has taken the lead, funding over 100 such funds in some 57 countries.

The essential idea is that the social fund provides finance and technical assistance in low-income communities, while those living in the communities are expected, selecting from competing contractors, to decide on how the money is to be spent, in carrying out investment activities. The core of the activity is expected to be some sort of public works, with an emphasis on development and infrastructure — water, sewage, transport, health-care facilities and so on.

The main claims in favour of social funds have been that they can moderate the risks faced by low-income communities while enabling the poor to decide more freely on how to spend the financial resources. It has also been argued that they help communities recover from social or economic shocks and are flexible because they are controlled at the local level.

Despite high levels of investment, most social funds were not designed to deal well with systemic shocks and, owing mostly to limited funding and inadequate planning, had only marginal effects on poverty reduction (Cornia, 1999).

Although social funds in some countries have been shown to benefit the very poor, the targeting involved in most social funds has been much less than perfect. For instance, in both Nicaragua and Peru, social funds were based on geographical targeting, which identified extremely poor communities reasonably well, but not all of the poorest households (Coady, 2004; Paxson and Schady, 2002). Other analyses have found that social funds typically have high exclusion and inclusion errors, supporting many who are not in need and failing to support many who are (Stewart and van der Geest, 1994), and have a poor record in terms of gender equity (Sabates-Wheeler and Kabeer, 2003).

Recent assessments of social funds for community-driven development by the World Bank indicate high ratings in development effectiveness, higher sustainability and stronger institutional development as compared with other Bank-wide averages.

Nevertheless, despite the favourable World Bank assessments, social funds are no longer seen as a powerful mechanism for community development and as a means of generating sustainable livelihoods. Increasingly, those funds have focused on supply-side improvements, shifting from public infrastructure to "human capital" development schemes.

Micro-insurance and microcredit schemes

Microfinance and microcredit have become hugely popular as development tools; they are strongly supported by the United Nations, and are promoted within the International Labour Organization by its Social Finance Programmes. In 2006, the Nobel Peace Prize was given to the founder of the Grameen Bank, the pioneering microcredit scheme for Bangladesh. Examples also exist across Africa, Asia, inner cities of the United States of America and, most recently, Eastern Europe. The "common minimum programme" of the Government of India includes a commitment to expand microcredit.

The primary feature of microcredit schemes is the provision of small loans to the poor and vulnerable, as start-up capital for small business activity. They have been seen as assisting people in setting up microenterprises or in becoming self-employed. Group lending is encouraged, and the outstanding aspect has been the heavy orientation towards lending to women.

Their advocates have claimed that microcredit schemes encourage participatory involvement, and are self-targeting and empowering. Some schemes appear to have a good record in respect of reimbursement; others much less so. Crucially, for those concerned with the promotion of livelihoods, they have been seen as a means of tying people over during periods of economic difficulty, thereby providing informal insurance, as well as of preventing a collapse of some small-scale businesses and a drift into unemployment.

Access to financial services by the poor is very important for their economic and social empowerment. As pointed out in the United Nations "Blue Book" (United Nations, 2006h,) on building inclusive financial sectors:

> "Creation and expansion of financial services targeted to poor and low-income populations can play a vital role in enhancing financial access. Inclusive financial sectors — those in which no segment of the population is excluded from accessing financial services — can contribute to attaining the goals contained in the United Nations Millennium Declaration, such as halving the proportion of people in the world who live in extreme poverty by 2015" (p. 4).

It has been proved that microfinance helps create jobs, empower women and reduce vulnerability. It not only facilitates increase of their incomes by the poor, but also helps enhance productivity in agriculture and informal urban economy sectors, thus contributing to the equitable distribution of the benefits of economic growth.

The main criticisms of microcredit schemes concern their sustainability, limited scope and difficulties with management. Some consider them to be too small to deal with systemic shocks and risks. They may also create the dependency of the near-poor on a series of small loans (Kabeer, 2001).

There is also concern about their ability to reach the very poor, since those working in what has been called the "mini economy" require such small amounts of money that even the microcredit institutions cannot handle the sums, owing to standardized administrative and monitoring costs (Matin, Hulme and Rutherford, 1999). There are some efforts under way, however, to correct these deficiencies and improve microfinance targeting so as to provide income-generating assets and prospects of self-employment to the very poorest.

Microfinance helps create employment among women and empowers them to generate and control their own income. Some concerns have been raised, however, that it may put women under more pressure by inducing them to overextend their work commitments (Goetz and Sen Gupta, 1996; Rahman, 1999).

Finally, many observers have questioned whether microcredit institutions are sustainable without the large donor assistance they have long been receiving. Moreover, it appears that there has been a drifting away from "group lending with joint liability" as originally conceived towards conventional individual lending and, in the process, away from a focus on the poorest and most economically insecure.

Food for work

Food for work is a direct measure to boost employment and respond to emergency needs. It has been an instrument of State policy all over the world for quite some time. Some countries have relied heavily on food-for-work schemes. In Ethiopia, for example, the Government has devoted 80 per cent of its food assistance to such projects.

The primary claim is that such schemes effectively target the poor, since they are self-selecting that, and like all direct employment measures of the workfare kind, they are relatively easy to legitimize among the middle class, who can see people working for their food. It is also argued that such schemes can be focused relatively easily on predetermined vulnerable groups, notably women. Indeed, the World Food Programme (WFP), which has been a major driver of food-for-work schemes, has required Governments to make women the major beneficiaries.

The main shortcoming of food-for-work schemes is that those engaged in what is often onerous labour end up burning more calories than are gained through the food given to them. The schemes may actually be detrimental to participants' health (Quisumbing, 2003; Osmani, 1997). Also, food-for-work projects can be inefficient and plagued by corruption. Moreover, food-for-work schemes may create disincentives for people to grow their own food, and may thus have a detrimental effect on long-term livelihoods.

Another peculiar feature of food-for-work schemes is that typically, women's share of the jobs obtained has been larger than that for similar cash-for-work schemes. This has been the case in Lesotho and Zambia, for instance (Subbarao, 2003). One interpretation is that food compensation is more gender-equitable. On the other hand, this feature may reflect the stigmatization effect of food as a form of compensation, which discourages men from participating. Food compensation may nevertheless be more gender-equitable inasmuch as the benefits for families are shared to a greater degree.

Food-for-work schemes may not be the most appropriate policy for promoting livelihoods or decent work. They are more consistent with charity than with the extension of human rights. Nevertheless, they attempt to lift people out of the hunger trap. In poverty-stricken communities hit by natural or man-made disasters, they may offer the only means to rebuild infrastructure and feed people at the same time.

Cash-for-work schemes

Cash-for-work projects, like food-for-work schemes, set out to combine poverty relief and employment generation, but are faster to implement and more cost-effective. They often involve "quick-impact projects" in disaster-affected areas, mobilizing communities to undertake rehabilitation efforts and offering people an immediate source of income. By providing cash, rather than specific food items, they allow recipients greater autonomy with respect to how they spend their earnings. In Aceh province in Indonesia, cash-for-work programmes enabled displaced populations to return and rebuild their communities in the aftermath of the tsunami.

Another example is the cash-for-work project operated in north-east Turkana in Kenya under the direction of Oxfam in 2001 and 2003. The primary objective was to assist in livelihood recovery, food security, skills transfer and local community empowerment, through projects to improve basic infrastructure. Oxfam staff concluded that the approach was more cost-effective than food-for-work schemes, producing higher multiplier effects on incomes in the local economies; but the administrative overheads were significant, which led them to conclude that larger cash transfers were needed, because food was not enough of an inducement to ensure efficient labour, and that more people in the community needed assistance than were actually involved in the work compensated by food handouts.

It was also concluded that the "sustainability of community projects was not always clear cut" and that there was a need to rethink suitability of projects that require hard labour" (Lothike, 2005), mainly because, as the available workforce in the area had consisted mainly of women, the additional demands placed on them while working on these projects "overburdened already difficult livelihoods". Thus, project identification should be more gender-sensitive, and labour-intensive projects may not always be appropriate.

Public works

Public works programmes have developed into a major policy instrument for employment-creation in situations of high or chronic unemployment and under-employment, as well as for minimizing consumption shortfalls in times of crises such as famine or drought. As social policy, public works are often presented as *self-selecting* or *self-targeting*, since, it is claimed, only those who are desperately in need of income will offer to work on public works projects. Public works projects create public goods, such as local infrastructure and schools, and have a political purpose in that they relieve social discontent through highly visible projects show-ing immediate results and raising the poor above a certain poverty line.

Public works have become central to some Governments' anti-poverty pro-grammes. In Chile in 1983, they provided 13 per cent of total employment; in Botswana in 1985-1986, they accounted for 21 per cent of the labour force; and in India in 1995, the public works scheme known as the Jawahar Rojgar Yojuna programme was supposed to have provided 1 billion person-days of labour (Subbarao and others, 1997). Often, the schemes have been introduced as a temporary measure, following an emergency or economic shock. For example, the public works scheme in Brazil known as the North-east Work Front Pro-gramme was implemented for two years (1998-2000) (Rocha, 2000).

The most famous public works scheme is the Maharashtra Employment Guarantee Scheme in India, which had been set up in the early 1970s and is still operating, although it peaked in the 1980s. Drawing in part on the Maharashtra Scheme, in 2005, the Government of India launched its most ambitious public works scheme, known as the National Rural Employment Guarantee scheme, by which the Government "guaranteed" employment to the rural poor (see box VI.2). Under this, initiative the Government made a commitment to provide 100 days of employment per year to each poor household in 200 districts, with the intention of rolling out the scheme to the whole country.

Box VI.2
The National Rural Employment Guarantee scheme in India

The National Rural Employment Guarantee Act in India ensures 100 days of employment per year to one unemployed member of every rural household. People employed by the scheme mostly work on infrastructure projects, such as construction of roads and water irrigation projects. Ninety per cent of the costs are covered by the central Government and 10 per cent by the state. The programme is designed to use manual unskilled labour rather than machines and prohibits the use of contractors.

Its main objectives are to uphold the right to work, reduce poverty and limit rural-urban migration of labourers. Workers are to be paid the statutory minimum wage applicable to agricultural workers. At the designated worksite, safe drinking water, access to on-site childcare (since the project aims for 60–70 per cent female participation) and first aid should be provided.

The Act will not be extended, as planned, until a review has been carried out to assess the results. There is a considerable gap between demand and supply in employment.

Critics have also questioned the process by which funds were allocated from the central Government to the States, and the claim of uniformity of wages, and have expressed the fear that the scheme will not generate valuable public assets.

Monitoring surveys have shown low awareness of the scheme among the rural poor, delays in issuance of job cards and discrimination in the registration process. It has been also demonstrated that work can be prioritized, with higher priority given, for example, to irrigation and land development, than to the construction of roads.

The success of the programme is linked to the new Indian Right to Information Act, giving every individual the right to request and receive information on how public money is being spent. It is hoped that this Act will be used by citizens' groups to monitor the effectiveness of the NREGA and will make it easier to expose corruption and the limitations of the scheme , thereby ensuring its improvement.

Public works can act as a sort of social insurance or, more correctly, social assistance. If the economically insecure knew that such jobs were available, or would become available in the seasonally slack period or expanded if there was an economic recession, they could be expected to have a greater degree of economic security. It has been shown that farmers living in the region covered by the Employment Guarantee Scheme in the State of Maharashtra were more likely to invest in higher-yielding, riskier varieties of seed than farmers living in neighbouring States (Department for International Development, 2006).

Box VI.3
Battling exceptionally high unemployment in
South Africa through public works

Faced with chronically high unemployment and income inequality, in 1994, the new Government of South Africa had made a commitment to use public works extensively. It launched a series of such projects — the National Public Works Programme, the Community-based Public Works Programme and the Special Public Works Programme. However, although they had generated about 4 million workdays in a year at one stage, this corresponded to a fraction of what was needed to make a serious dent in unemployment (McCord, 2003).

Still the trade unions and the Government were united in pressing for more public works, even though they were proving costly and rather ineffectual, as had all previous efforts (Standing, Sender and Weeks, 1996). So, in late 2004, an "Expanded" Public Works Programme was set up. Although the Expanded Programme used targeting so as to include women, youth and people with disabilities, the jobs created were short-term, concentrated in labour-intensive, low-productivity activities and involved little or no skill development lasting effects. By 2006, the outlook was pessimistic (McCord, 2005b).

Significantly, in 2002, the Government had negotiated a Code of Practice for Special Public Works Programmes with the Congress of South African Trade Unions stipulating that wages should be just below the minimum in the relevant sector and area. Ironically, this turned out to be higher than the actual earnings in many areas of the country, so that a large proportion of the temporary jobs were taken by those who were not among the poorest and were often engaged other forms of non-wage activity as well.

Public works create valuable infrastructure and enhance productive capacities through land development projects such as irrigation and prevention of soil erosion that may have a high economic return through increased agricultural output. They can result in the construction of roads or in better water supplies, as was the case for a public works scheme in Arba Minch, Ethiopia (Benn, 2006). Not always, though, are the results sustainable, durable or more efficient than other those obtained through means aimed at producing such infrastructure. The outputs may be less durable when the objective of maximizing employment leads to highly labour-intensive methods dependent on unskilled and ill trained labour (see box VI.3).

A related criticism of public works is that they tend to be predominantly short-term "make-work" schemes. The productivity is low, and the labour is temporary, so that they do not provide either value for money or sustainable employment. The inefficiency is compounded by high administrative and monitoring costs, so that the proportion of the funds devoted to public works that actually goes to the intended beneficiaries is cut severely. It is generally estimated that of all forms of social protection, public works have the highest administrative costs as a share of total expenditure.

It is also clear that often there are large-scale substitution effects and deadweight effects. In other words, public works may merely displace other workers doing the work for private firms or they may entail the undertaking of a project that would have been carried out anyway.

It is also claimed that the degree of effective targeting is, in practice, very limited. Although the usual objective is to provide labour for the poorest and for the unemployed in greatest financial need, numerous studies have found that this is not what usually happens. One obvious shortcoming is that public works schemes discriminate against labour-constrained households. Another is that those living far from the worksites have the greatest difficulty in benefiting from the available work opportunities. Moreover, those with disabilities are the least likely to be able to do the work on offer. Women, in particular, are frequently penalized, because often they are subject to severe time pressures owing to their other work demands in and around the home.

However, even if the public works do succeed in exclusively targeting the poor, they may create poverty traps, with all the moral hazards that those traps entail. In very poor communities, the poor and vulnerable will then have an interest in staying just below the poverty line or at least appearing to do so.

Some critics have claimed that public works are stigmatizing, while some advocates have suggested that this is actually a desirable feature in that thereby only those most desperately in need are encouraged to apply. While accurate targeting through self-selection may be desirable, achieving it by lowering wages is objectionable in the context of decent work.

Another common criticism is that public works favour men, who receive a disproportionate number of the jobs. This could be countered by design changes. Indeed, if women are historically disadvantaged in the labour market through cultural barriers or discriminatory prejudices, public works could be used as a lever with which to break down the barriers. Some public works projects have attempted to recruit women for traditionally male jobs, thus initiating a process of change in the rigid division of labour between men and women. Although the record in this regard is mixed, public works have a potential for promoting gender equality.

For example, in the South African Zibambele (doing it for ourselves) scheme, employment contracts were given to the household unit, rather than to individuals. In addition, recruiters focused on female-headed households, and worksites were located near the home of potential worker participants. As a result, 93 per cent of participants were women (McCord, 2004; Samson, van Niekerk and MacQuene, 2006). Another way to ensure women's participation is through including women in the planning process, especially for publicly supported community works projects.

Similarly, India's new National Rural Employment Guarantee scheme has established anti-discrimination provisions, access to on-site childcare and worksites close to the homes of potential participants (Right to Food Campaign, 2005). On the other hand, despite the fact that similar provisions were included in the long-running Maharashtra Employment Guarantee Scheme, it still has only a minority of women among its participants, even though many more women have traditionally been registered in the scheme (Gaiha and Imai, 2005).

Another controversy centres on the wages paid for those doing public works. Many supporters believe they should pay decent wages, or the market wage rate, while others argue that they should pay at or even below the minimum wage, as a means of self-selecting the poor, which has been a common tendency. Often, the wage is determined by that prevailing for agricultural manual labour, and some economists have said that this should be the case (Ravallion, 1999); others have said the pay should be below the market wage (Subbarao, 2003; Hirway and Terhal, 1994).

Indeed, the Maharashtra Scheme long maintained its claim to being a "guarantee" of work for all those applying by limiting participation through the offer of a low minimum wage. Once the courts had ruled that it must pay the official minimum wage, and particularly after the minimum wage went up, it had to ration work, thereby ceasing to offer a "guarantee" (Subbarao, 2003). On the other hand, one of the most positive features of the Maharashtra Scheme has been its ability to stabilize the incomes of the poor by ensuring 100 days of work per year to all job seekers (Dev, 1995).

· As with other cash-for-work schemes, setting the wage below subsistence flouts the principles underlying minimum wage laws and may intensify poverty

(McCord, 2005b). Moreover, if the objective of paying subsubsistence wages is to induce self-targeting, the result may be the opposite of what was intended, because it may indicate that only those with access to some other source of income could afford to take the low-paying public works jobs. Most perversely of all, paying subsubsistence wages may actually worsen the poverty of the participants if they are induced to give up other forms of work, which may disrupt structured livelihood systems in local communities.

For the public projects in Malawi, the wage was set at the equivalent of US$ 0.30 per day. An evaluation study commissioned by the Government found that the very low wages were ineffective in selecting the very poor, while the low payments left participants exposed to greater poverty as a result of the hard manual labour which raised their requirements, thereby increasing their risk of malnutrition and their need for health care (Chirwa and others, 2004). Members of poor labour-constrained households may be unable to take very low wage jobs because in doing so, they would have to give up other essential domestic and subsistence activities.

Paying low wages on public works also tends to lower the average wage in other jobs in low-income areas. Perversely, this could result in more widespread impoverishment, since lower wages for individual workers may mean that families would have subsubsistence incomes. In a few cases, the authorities have deliberately cut other wages so as to finance public works.

Compounding the problem caused by setting low wages is the fact that many public works schemes have been dilatory in paying workers, reflecting the slackness of regulatory control. In some cases, delays in payment have gone on for months, resulting in indebtedness and considerable local distress (ibid.).

The debate centring around wages in public works leads to one crucial conclusion. Countries where wages are bolstered by some regulatory device, such as a minimum wage or national collective bargaining, are not suited to the establishment of large-scale public works schemes intended to be a form of social protection.

Another criticism is that public works are very prone to political capture, through which powerful politicians ensure that the schemes are located in their areas, even though those may not be among the poorest. Alongside such tendencies, there is likely to be bureaucratic capture, with local bureaucrats' taking a financial cut derived from their allocation of work opportunities.

Ultimately, these tendencies show that there is usually considerable discretionary decision-making.

However, the most damning criticism of public works is that they tend not to benefit the poorest and most economically insecure. Even the Maharashtra Scheme was found to have failed in this respect. Some other schemes may have fared somewhat better, but there can be little doubt that the leakages are substantial, owing to ineffective targeting and administration, corruption and simple errors.

Still, public works may represent a significant response to unemployment and poverty, while creating valuable infrastructure, if they are appropriately designed as far as targeting, scale, wage level, duration of employment and effects on long-term development are concerned. Small in scale and temporary in nature, public works often address unemployment only as a transient phenomenon, ignoring its structural features, but they may still stimulate the production of second-order economic benefits through the infusion of cash into the local economy, thus supporting private sector job-creation (McCord, 2004).

In conclusion, while public works may successfully address transitory crises and threats to livelihoods, political considerations do often overtly influence choice and location. To improve their effectiveness, the wage rate should be set at a relatively high level so as to ensure social protection without causing labour-market distortions. Programmes should generate productive assets benefiting the poor, and it is the poorest who should be targeted. Local governments should be empowered in respect of planning and managing the projects. Moreover, the work schedule should be harmonized with the survival requirements of the poorest households so that caregivers can undertake household activities. Ideally, public works programmes should establish long-term employment prospects for the poorest so that they can lift themselves out of poverty (McCord, 2005b; Ravallion, 1999; Subbarao and others, 1997).

Concluding remarks

Special job-creation measures appeal to politicians because by introducing them they portray themselves as being actively engaged in addressing unemployment and labour market failure. That does not mean that these are the best or even the least bad-options. Much depends on the impact of the sacrifice of other measures and on the indirect effects of these direct schemes, which often are inefficient and result in a waste of public funds.

Different schemes are suitable to different circumstances and involve different levels of administrative and monitoring costs. A common requirement, however, is that every scheme practice proper targeting so as to reach the poor, which would include sensitivity to gender considerations in order to encourage the active participation of women. Since public resources are used to pay for these schemes, efficiency and effectiveness of projects are always a concern. Important lessons have been learned from projects in many countries.

The extensive examination of public works in this chapter leads to the conclusion that they are best suited to emergency situations, as interventions designed to help in restructuring after some economic shock or slump. Yet, even in this role, they tend to be poor and inefficient mechanisms for providing universal economic security. It is doubtful whether they can be conducted on a substantial scale in most countries. Even when established on the scale of India's national scheme, they are certainly not a panacea for the problem of how to generate decent work and full employment in developing countries.

Similarly, other demand-side measures to create employment, as implemented so far, have not been sufficient to achieve the objectives of the decent work agenda despite their positive impacts in terms of both poverty reduction and the provision of a degree of economic security against shocks and other emergencies. A more comprehensive approach which could include some of the existing demand-side measures, rather than one narrowly focusing on employment creation, is needed to promote decent work for all.

Chapter VII

Policy priorities for employment and decent work

If dignified or decent work is to become more than a slogan, it must encompass much more than the call for a greater numbers of jobs of any kind. "Full employment" and "decent work" are conflicting concepts, to the extent that there will always likely be a trade-off between quantity and quality. Generating employment, albeit desirable in itself, must be consistently undertaken with respect for decent working conditions.

Jobs are only part of the work and livelihood of people in any society. As the twenty-first century progresses, it is important to treat all forms of work, including unpaid care and voluntary community work, as equally legitimate. This notion is gradually influencing reforms of social security systems and labour laws.

A key challenge concerns the need to enhance basic socio-economic security for all, which necessarily leads to questions about priorities and trade-offs. Policymakers must decide what types of security are most fundamental for the flourishing of decent work. One of the basic discontents with globalization has been caused by worker insecurity, which affects middle-class as well as working-class people in even the richest economies of the world. While much attention has been devoted to this phenomenon in the developed world, it has also become a source of political concern in rapidly growing developing economies, in spite of high levels of economic growth. The fact that the absence of security for workers appears to endanger social harmony poses a major challenge in terms of the future of work and labour.

The need for voice

An essential aspect of any kind of work activity, is what is often referred to as "voice". Voice refers to the political engagement of workers in shaping their work and work conditions (Hirschman, 1970). Without voice, both as individuals and as members of collective bodies bargaining with employers and other authorities, workers cannot influence outcomes and assure decent or better work. Voice is contrasted with "exit" options, the more usual way of expressing discontent when bargaining capacities are too weak to induce beneficial changes. Without voice, workers have few options other than opting out of their work situation or reluctantly accepting it for fear of the alternatives. In times of high unemployment, or in situations where labour markets are structured in ways that penalize voluntary exit strategies, workers have to put up with poor conditions or low incomes or risk the welfare of their families. Having voice alters that position.

Labour laws were usually fashioned in accordance with the situation of workers in a fixed worksite who were in what has been called the standard employment relationship, that is to say, a direct long-term employment relationship involving a legally recognized employee status. This guided the development of labour standards and labour law throughout the twentieth century. As it has become increasingly clear that most workers are outside the standard norm, policymakers have tried to extend equal treatment to categories of non-standard labour. In doing so, they have tended to preserve the idea of a standard norm, without recognizing the diversity of work patterns and the significance of forms of work outside the notion of employment. Clearly, this approach does not embrace the idea of work in its broader meaning.

Aside from securing minimum standards for people doing all forms of work, perhaps the biggest challenge for workers in the twenty-first century is recognizing the need for and developing new forms of voice in response to the difficult realities of open, flexible labour markets and the exertions of pressure to undertake various forms of work. Clearly, workers around the world are not participating more in the traditional form of worker representation, namely, trade unions.

It has been easy to be critical of unions as they tried to come to terms with globalization, labour market re-regulation and economic liberalization. They appear to be out of touch in trying to obstruct change and restore the benefits for workers they were instrumental in gaining during the twentieth century. However, the criticism should be muted, since workers of all sorts need organizations that can represent them and their interests. Governments and employers also need to be pressured to ensure that they do not neglect such interests and aspirations. Independent workers' associations are essential for decent work, even if some need to change their ways.

Part of the necessary reorganization in respect of having voice encompasses institutional governance, entailing the need to give work greater priority in social policymaking and policy evaluation. Viable institutions include national councils for work and negotiated social compacts between workers' bodies, employers and Governments. Here, too, old models are unlikely to suffice. Fortunately, there is an associational revolution taking place, with thousands of new forms of civil society groups trying to come to terms with new challenges. Many may be flawed but, overall, they reflect a continuing desire to better the world, including the world of work.

Informalization and the response

Economic informalization is sweeping the world, yet the term "informalization" has a double connotation. In its negative sense, informalization implies the lack of legal recognition and social protection of work done outside the remit of protective labour regulations and social security. In its positive sense, informalization connotes the possession of meaningful autonomy and the ability to make decisions without external control including on when and how much to work.

Labour-market flexibility and other processes of economic liberalization mean that many more workers are in relatively informal statuses. And there is no prospect that there will be changes in this regard, even if policymakers should wish to implement them. Social and labour-market policies have to adapt to these current and prospective realities. Workers of any status require basic economic security in order to be able to make rational decisions that can enhance the decency of their work and the meaningfulness of their livelihoods.

The most important needs for workers in informal status are basic income security and basic voice security (International Labour Organization, 2004a). In an earlier chapter, it was indicated how small-scale cash transfers are enabling economically insecure and poor people in difficult social circumstances to restore their livelihoods and become socially productive; but even here, decent livelihoods will emerge only if organizations represent the development related interests and needs of such workers. The dilemma, put simply, is whether to promote the informal sector as a provider of employment and incomes or to seek to extend regulation and social protection to include this sector, and thereby possibly reduce its capacity to provide jobs and incomes for an ever-expanding labour force.

Strengthening representation is one need. Even more fundamentally though, policymakers should rethink the nature of labour law in the context of the long-term drift towards more flexible and informal economic activities. There is a need to formalize, in the sense that it is undesirable to leave informal workers unprotected and without the labour entitlements deemed basic to other workers. Some commentators believe that regulations and labour law should be discriminatory, in other words, less onerous for informal employers. This is inequitable and likely to lead to moves by some employers to informalize so as to avoid taxes and coverage by labour laws. More attractively, the cost of legalizing informal activities should be reduced, provided this reduction is universal.

In this regard, the legislation and regulations should not discourage those making valuable products or services in the informal sector from continuing to do so. They must be neither too complex nor too costly, since if they were, this would cause some to cease production and some to go underground, resulting in even more onerous and unpleasant working conditions. As one sensible reform, all businesses should be required to formally register with the authorities in a simple and low-cost manner, since only if they are registered can the rule of law and labour protection function. In the same vein, the assets of those producing informally should be registered as entrepreneurial property, thus providing proper legal status to those assets (Fuentes, 1997).

Whether formal or informal, there should be a campaign to ensure that there are written labour or employment contracts for all workers. In practice, only those with written agreements can be effectively protected by labour or common law. In some countries, the vast majority of those working in informal activities do not have written contracts and thus are not protected by labour legislation. Simple written contracts, setting out the basic conditions of pay and working arrangements, should not be seen as excessive. It is a necessary, if not sufficient condition for turning informal labour into decent labour.

Labour rights revisited

The right to work

For several hundred years, there has been a running debate centred on the right to work, but it has proved hard to define such a right, let alone show how it could be implemented. Surely, it cannot refer to the right to a job, since this would mean imposing an obligation on an "employer" to give anybody a job or to maintain it once it has been created. Suppose that employers had to lay off workers in order to continue in business. It would scarcely be fair to regard them as culpable for having denied the right to work.

Conversely, the term cannot refer to the right to have any job one chooses. Nor could a market economy function on the basis of everybody's having a "right to work" guaranteed by government. Moreover, while creating jobs for more people might please government planners, it could actually erode the capacity of people to pursue dignifying livelihoods.

The right to work can mean only the right of people everywhere to pursue their livelihoods in freely chosen activities. Traditionally, the notion of full employment, as enshrined in International Labour Convention No. 122 concerning Employment Policy Convention, has encompassed the crucial term "freely chosen". Workfare schemes come perilously close to denying that freedom and, as such, may not be consistent with the advancement of social, economic and cultural rights.

Economic security as a right

The concept of the right to basic economic security is gaining respectability. People in all types of society cannot be expected to pursue a life of work unless their lives are grounded in basic social and economic security. Two complementary principles are at stake, namely, of universalism and social solidarity. With globalization, inequalities and insecurities have undermined both of these principles. Universalism means that all people in society must have the same minimal standard set of rights, regardless of their age, sex, work status, marital or family status, race, religion or migrant status. A universal right to feel secure is among the most fundamental objectives in this regard. Only if there is basic economic security can an individual feel socially responsible, and only if that is provided can policymakers expect citizens to act in socially responsible ways.

Universal schemes of security are fundamentally market-neutral, that is to say, they do not introduce market distortions and therefore have relatively little effect on competitiveness. They are simple to administer and low-cost, and there is little scope for bureaucratic abuse, discretionary behaviour or petty corruption. The benefits are non-stigmatizing, and being universal, help strengthen social solidarity, including community and social cohesion, and may even assist in developing a sense of national pride. Above all, universal economic security fosters full freedom. In such circumstances, decent work could flourish.

Unfortunately, however, the dominant discourse at present is still in favour of targeting, selectivity and conditional benefits for the deserving poor. Yet, the efficiency and equity of selective interventions can be questioned. Social solidarity is harder to envisage in societies facing widening inequalities and social stratification, but without a sense of social solidarity, social tensions mount, and the demand that the losers and the disadvantaged behave in ways that meet the expectations of the winners becomes ineffective and unfair. The safest way to overcome the social divide that these widening inequalities create is to enhance the voices of all interests in society equally.

In this regard, we are living in fascinating times. An associational revolution is taking place, and it is having an enormous effect on work patterns across the world. There are many who regret the decline in the strength of trade unions, since there should be no doubt that they have acted as powerful instruments for improving working conditions and for fostering the according of dignity and social protection to workers across the world; but we must acknowledge that they have less broad appeal for those working in the twenty first century. In most countries, unionization rates have declined and show no signs of being reversed. Partly, this reflects the labourist orientation of unions and their leaderships. Nowadays, many more people see themselves as citizens first and identify themselves with their interests outside the jobs they are doing at any particular moment. Hence, more people are joining organizations that represent them in terms of what they are most interested in, beyond the realm of their work. Still, work remains central to the lives of almost everybody, and representative organizations are essential to ensuring that working conditions are more than just adequate and that social and economic rights are recognized and understood.

Social protection systems also need to adapt to more flexible labour-market conditions in order to provide economic security to all workers. With more and more workers in employment situations that are casual, informal and outside of standard collective contracts, by choice or by necessity, universality of coverage becomes even more important. In addition, the broadening of the concept of work to include unpaid work demands new thinking with regard to eligibility for, and contributions required in order to participate in, social protection systems.

The new international labour market and social groups

In the ongoing global transformation, a new international labour market is emerging, which is placing unprecedented demands on international and national policymakers, requiring that they to adapt to new flexibilities and insecurities. Certain priorities are becoming clearer. Thus, old statutory labour regulations have proved fragile and controversial, even among those observers wishing to see workers' conditions and livelihoods steadily improving. Old mechanisms of distribution have also been failing, and the traditional means of pursuing social protection have been found wanting.

Expectations of greater participation

For all social groups, there has been a movement towards greater labour-force participation around the world. Many groups are increasingly ready and able to take part in work, however defined. Younger cohorts in society are staying longer in education, and fewer are engaged in exploitative forms of child labour; but while young people's entry into the labour force is delayed, their expectations are too often frustrated, paradoxically at a time when they are better prepared than before. At the other end of the age spectrum, older workers expect to stay longer in the labour force; sometimes this will be out of necessity, and often by choice. Yet, the prospects of greater participation in the labour force remain lower for persons with disabilities and for indigenous peoples, who have traditionally been on the fringes of the labour market. While there are certainly hopeful signs that their rights and needs are being acknowledged, many challenges remain for the greater participation of these groups.

In most societies, it has been in the area of gender that the most progress towards greater participation can be reported, but where at the same time, the largest inequalities among people have persisted. Too often, progress that allowed for full and equal participation of women in the labour force experienced setbacks allowing significant inequalities between women and men to continue. A similarly mixed track record of progress and setbacks can be observed for migrants: while they have become an established (but underappreciated) part of the global workforce, their rights and needs still need much greater attention. These developments have reinforced inequalities, not only between these social groups and "mainstream" society, but also among the groups themselves.

Migrant workers

As emphasized earlier in this report, we are in the midst of a global transformation characterized by the slow emergence of an international labour market. International labour mobility is growing and will continue to grow. Thus far, across the world, the needs of migrant workers have received inadequate consideration, and it is regrettable that political democratization has not ensured greater attention to those needs. One indicator of the seriousness of the problem is the fact that the International Labour Organization has found it hard to persuade its member Governments to ratify its main conventions concerning migrant workers.

The lack of agreement on what should constitute migrant workers' rights has several adverse effects, not only on migrant workers and their families but on other groups of workers as well. As the international labour market continues to evolve, this issue demands very high priority. There is a need for countries to uphold the human rights of migrants, especially those rights enshrined in the seven core United Nations human rights treaties (Global Commission on International Migration, 2005). In addition, developing countries, faced with a skills exodus, need to improve working conditions in public employment, invest more in research and development, and help identify job opportunities at home for returning migrants with advanced education. The World Bank, among others, also suggests managed migration programmes, including temporary work visas for low-skilled migrants in industrialized countries, which could help alleviate problems associated with irregular migration and allow increased movement of temporary workers.

Disability and work rights

Many millions of people across the world have to overcome physical or intellectual disabilities as they seek to work their way through life. How a society responds to the plight of persons with disabilities reflects and helps define its culture. With open, more flexible and more informal labour markets, persons with disabilities could easily continue to be marginalized and chronically disadvantaged. Rather than just focus on increasing the "employability" of persons with disabilities – however beneficial that might be – policies and labour practices should increase their emphasis on making workplaces more suitable for workers with disabilities. This will include, for instance, ensuring that reasonable accommodation is provided to persons with disabilities in the workplace, introducing flexible working hours so that they can attend to their medical needs, and making workplace communications accessible for those confronting visual, aural or intellectual difficulties.

Older workers and lifetime flexibility

The traditional industrial model of a life cycle — a short period of "schooling" followed by a relatively long period of "economic activity" and employment followed in turn by a rather short period of "retirement" — is breaking down all over the world as a result of longevity. The challenge is not just to enable older workers to keep their jobs. In essence, it is far more a matter of enabling older people to combine leisure and work in flexible ways, in accordance with their needs, aspirations and changing capacities. One may be confident that the conventional progression of school-work-retirement will gradually wither away as the twenty-first century progresses. This may seem far fetched for developing countries; but it is possible that as members of affluent communities in those countries become integrated with their peers in developed countries, a new form of social dualism will emerge. There will be a privileged minority that moves flexibly in and out of labour-force activities during the course of their adult lives without a predetermined pattern of employment followed by full-time retirement. In developed countries, that flexibility could very well become the norm. At present, social and regulatory policies are ill adapted to the needs arising from that pattern of life.

Improving the working conditions of women

Women have made inroads of varying extents to the labour markets of all regions. However, increased employment of women has not necessarily been accompanied by their socio-economic empowerment. When support with respect to care work is provided, specifically when childcare is readily available, women tend to have more autonomy in choosing whether or not to work outside the home. Where policies support maternity and paternity leave, and are flexible for women returning to work after childbearing, including the availability of part-time work, more women work outside of the home. Many millions of women are suffering from "overemployment", and social policies should seek to reduce the domestic burden rather than force them into engaging in more labour activity without addressing the structural factors that result in their overwork. Policymakers need to focus not just on preventing discrimination in hiring practices, but also on post-hiring training and induction processes.

Channelling young people's expectations

One could argue that young people are winners in globalization, particularly those able to use their competitive advantage in technology-related employment. Achievements in both basic and higher education by young men and, increasingly, young women have created a larger, better-educated generation. This has directly resulted in higher expectations among young people when they enter the world of work. Unfortunately, in many cases, the economies in which they live have been unable to absorb the large group of well-educated students.

Policy priorities for moving forward

The challenges for decent work in the twenty-first century are great. While traditional models and mechanisms for achieving voice representation, economic security and full employment are proving inadequate in the era of globalization and increased labour-market flexibility, new approaches are being explored. At this point, policy evolution is still in the early stages. The only certainty seems to be change. The international community and national Governments and their civil society partners need to work collaboratively to move forward the agenda of promoting productive and decent work for all that was set out at the World Summit for Social Development held in Copenhagen more than 10 years ago, and reaffirmed at the 2005 World Summit.

First, it is worth reiterating that decent work for all, rather than economic growth per se, or even simply creating jobs, should be placed at the centre of economic and social policy-making. This paradigm shift should be the starting point for the fundamental change that is needed. International institutions, especially those in the United Nations system, should actively promote the shift and incorporate the principle governing it in their own activities.

At the international level, cooperation and coordination among countries are needed to counteract the pressures of a "race to the bottom" in the global competition for investment and trade advantages. In this respect, the United Nations system, with the support and active participation of member States, should work to incorporate an internationally agreed floor of labour standards, together with environmental safeguards, into multilateral and regional trade agreements so as to protect the decency of work in all countries.

Sharing of experiences and international coordination of social and economic policies will also contribute to the exploration of means to meet the collective challenge of creating productive employment and decent work for all in the twenty-first century. The United Nations, especially the international financial institutions within the system, has been facilitating such exchanges and coordination and should continue to strengthen its role in this area.

At the national level, social and economic policies, and even institutions, need to adjust to the new realities and demands of a globalizing world. It is clear that some of the traditional institutions, such as trade unions and employment-based social protection that served labour well in the twentieth century, are facing challenges. It is critical that reform of social protection systems in developed countries and the expansion of such systems in developing countries aim at ensuring economic security for all in the more flexible labour market. The principles of universality and social solidarity, although questioned by some in the era of globalization and increasing reliance on market forces, actually seem to foster a better response to the challenges of the new employment and work situation.

In many countries, policy measures to reduce inequality should be pursued in conjunction with those aimed at stimulating economic growth in order to ensure a more equitable distribution of the benefits of growth, which has been shown to reduce poverty and create a more favourable socio-economic environment for sustaining long-term growth.

Traditional government-supported demand-side employment schemes also need to be rethought and put into the context of decent work, instead of being viewed simply as job-creation measures. Policy measures should also be implemented to further remove barriers to participation in the labour force and to facilitate access to decent work for all social groups, including those traditionally marginalized and excluded. All policy measures should take into consideration the ongoing demographic and social changes that are shaping the world of employment and work.

National conditions and capacities vary, hence there is no one-size-fits-all solution to the important issues at hand. The international community should provide support to national Governments in their endeavours, and international guidelines and principles of productive employment and decent work could serve as the foundation and framework for national policy.

The civil society and the private sector can also play an important role in promoting decent work for all. Indeed, the rollback in protective statutory regulations in the globalization era has been accompanied by a shift to self-regulation, with a renewed focus on employer voluntarism, as captured by numerous exhortations to enterprises to show corporate social responsibility and to adhere to voluntary codes of conduct.

Many international voluntary codes of conduct have built on the Guidelines for Multinational Enterprises of the Organization for Economic Cooperation and Development and the Tripartite Declaration of Principles concerning Multinational Enterprises and Social Policy of the International Labour Organization. Other codes of conduct for multinationals include the Global Sullivan Principles of Social Responsibility and Caux Round Table Principles for Business. The United Nations Global Compact, the Global Reporting Initiative, socially responsible investing, monitoring global supply chains and the fair trade movement are some examples of international and national initiatives promoting corporate social responsibility around the world.

While compliance and monitoring are still a challenge, voluntary corporate social responsibility and related reporting usually focused on environmental and social issues have witnessed rapid growth. In 2002, 45 per cent of the world's largest 250 companies produced reports on corporate social responsibility, up from 35 per cent in 1999 (KPMG, 2002). However, a set of agreed guidelines on what such reports should look like is still to be developed.

There is an impression that the corporate social responsibility reporting movement has made less progress on labour and work issues than on environmental and economic issues. As noted by the working party on the Social Dimension of Globalization of the Governing Body of the International Labour Office disclosure of information on labour and employment in this type of report is generally quite weak (International Labour Organization, 2003d, para. 21). In reviewing the issues that are most typically reported, it added that the subjects least frequently reported on included equal remuneration, job security, the effect of technology on employment quality and quantity, disciplinary practices and establishing linkages with national enterprises (ibid., para. 22).

Self-regulation undoubtedly has a place to play in the more liberalized world of business and labour relations that is emerging in the globalization era. Its limitations are also real. Thus, legislation and monitoring pressures are essential and should be required. Governments should intervene in support of corporate social responsibility, if only because there are positive externalities that individual companies may not be able to realize on their own (Hopkins, 1998; 2006).

Society depends on responsible behaviour to a much greater extent than can be captured by detailed legislation and complex regulations. In respect of shaping the evolving global governance, realism requires a balance between idealism and common practice. However, companies should not be expected to take over responsibility for social policy, and should avoid becoming paternalistic. At the core, business is about making profits, and public policy is the responsibility of States (Annan, 2001). Partnership between Governments and the private sector is necessary with regard to exploring means to promote corporate social responsibility as an instrument for the achievement of decent work for all.

Concluding remarks

It is in this, the twenty-first century, that economic, social and cultural rights should come into their own. The world has the resources, the wealth and the knowledge to make this a reality, if its leaders realize what economic globalization and international labour markets imply for workers across the globe.

Globalization entails more uncertainty and insecurity for workers and for communities that rely on work and labour to procure their livelihoods — in other words, for most people. There are benefits from economic liberalization, but at the same time there are powerful negative effects: large numbers of people are more insecure or face economic and social hardships as a direct result of the liberalization of economic and social policies and the dismantling of institutions and regulations built up before the onset of globalization.

With greater integration of the two most populous countries of the world, China and India, there is now increasingly a global labour force, in which the number of adults prepared and able to offer their labour has doubled. This has dramatically altered the bargaining position of capital and labour, of corporations and workers. The returns to capital and intellectual property rights have gone up, and the returns to financial capital investment may have gone up even more, leaving workers and working communities with a dwindling share of national and international income.

In those circumstances, it is unrealistic to expect that collective labour bargaining around wages will result in a surge of wage earnings. Policymakers have yet to come to terms with this reality, and have yet to devise strategies to check the growing inequalities of recent years (United Nations, 2005a). If decent work is to become the right its proponents wish it to be, then they have to address this functional income inequality at the global level.

In the course of its evolution, the human species has survived and flourished, because its members have shown a capacity for social cooperation. It is impossible, however, to sustain such solidarity without a shared sense of fairness. This social factor is not about more generous acts of charity, exemplified by a situation where the "winners" in globalization and economic liberalization would make the gesture of contributing more of their income and wealth to philanthropic causes. The world should not be dependent on such displays of pity, rather, it must function on the basis of respect for social, economic and cultural rights. These rights are insufficiently respected now, as reflected in growing inequalities in remuneration. Such disparities are hard to justify, since there is no evidence that they are necessary for reasons related either to incentive or to productivity.

Indeed, these economic, social and cultural rights are not being respected in those societies where large numbers of people are able only to survive, and only in degrading circumstances. Those rights can be respected only if people are able to make choices about their livelihoods and work, and if they can envisage a future in which they are able to improve their capabilities and human development through their work. In the end, work should be an important means of gaining self-respect, and dignity and achieving a reaffirmation of human identity. Where work does not have such a role — and far too often that is the case — policymakers should pause before introducing punitive social policies. Decent work is surely dignifying work and in order to be that, it must be grounded in basic economic security. The challenge is ultimately, about the distribution of opportunities, and rewards from productive activity.

Bibliography

Adams, Richard, Jr., and John Page (2005). Do international migration and remittances reduce poverty in developing countries? *World Development*, vol. 33, No. 10, pp. 1645-1669.

Alber, Jens, and Guy Standing (2000). Social dumping: catch-up or convergence? *Journal of European Social Policy*, vol.10, No. 2, pp. 99-119.

Albert, Bill (2006). Lessons from the Disability Knowledge and Research (KaR) Programme. The findings and broader lessons learned from the second phase of the Disability (KaR) Programme (2003-2005). Norwich, United Kingdom: Overseas Development Group, University of East Anglia; and London: Healthlink Worldwide.

Anker, Richard (2000). Conceptual and research frameworks for the economics of child labour and its elimination. International Labour Organization/International Programme on the Elimination of Child Labour (ILO/IPEC) Working Paper. Geneva: International Labour Office.

_____ (2006). Occupational segregation: lack of opportunities, inequality and discrimination. Paper presented at the United Nations Expert Group Meeting on Full Employment and Decent Work, 10-12 October, 2006, New York.

Annan, Kofi (2001). Broader social roles for business will complement search for profit, Secretary-General tells Swiss business community. Press release SG/SM/7756, United Nations, New York, 28 March. Available from *http://www.un.org/News/Press/docs/2001/sgsm7756.doc.htm* (accessed 21 June 2007).

Arup, Christopher, and others (2006). *Labour Law and Labour Market Regulation*. Riverwood, New South Wales, Australia: The Federation Press.

Atkinson, A.B. (2003). Income inequality in OECD countries: notes and explanations. Oxford, United Kingdom. Mimeo.

Attanasio, Orazio, Pinelop, Goldberg and Nina Pavcnik (2003). Trade reforms and wage inequality in Colombia. NBER Working Paper, No. 9830. Cambridge, Massachusetts: National Bureau of Economic Research. July.

Auer, Peter and Mariangels Fortuny (2000). *Ageing of the Labour Force in OECD Countries: Economic and Social Consequences*. Employment Paper No. 2000/2, Geneva: International Labour Office.

Autor, David H., Lawrence F. Katz and Melissa S. Kearney (2006). The polarization of the US labor market. NBER Working Paper, No.11986. Cambridge, Massachusetts: National Bureau of Economic Research. January.

Bartley, T. (2006). The private monitors of global trade. *International Herald Tribune*, 17 September.

Beattie, Alan (2006). Follow the thread. *Financial Times*, 22 July, p. 16.

Benn, Hilary (2006). Meeting our promises: basic services for everyone, everywhere. White Paper speech by the Secretary of State for International Development, 16 February. London.

Bernard, Andrew B., and J. Bradford Jensen (2002). The deaths of manufacturing plants. NBER Working Paper, No. 9026. Cambridge, Massachusetts: National Bureau of Economic Research. June.

Berry, Albert, and John Serieux (2001). Riding the elephants: the evolution of world economic growth and income distribution at the end of the 20th century (1980-2000). DESA working paper series, No. ST/ESA/2006/DWP/27. September.

Berthoud, Richard (2000). Ethnic employment penalties in Britain. *Journal of Ethnic and Migration Studies,* vol. 26, No. 3. (July).

Beyer, Harold, Patricio Rojas and Rodrigo Vergara (1999). Trade liberalization and wage inequality. *Journal of Development Economics,* vol. 59, No.1 (June), pp. 103-123.

Bhalotra, Sonia (2000). Is child work necessary? Typescript. Cambridge, United Kingdom, March.

Boeri, Tito, Daniela Del Boca and Christopher Pissarides (2005). *Women at Work: An Economic Perspective.* Oxford, United Kingdom: Oxford University Press.

Bollen, K.A. and R.W. Jackman (1995). Income inequality and democratization revisited. *American Sociological Review,* vol. 60, pp. 983-989.

Booth, A.L., M. Francesconi and J. Frank (2002). Temporary jobs: stepping stones or dead ends? *Economic Journal,* vol. 112, No. 480, pp. F181- F188.

Bourguignon, F., and C. Morrison (2002). Inequality among world citizens: 1820-1992. *American Economic Review,* vol. 92, No. 4 (September).

Boyden, J. and W. Myers (1995). Exploring alternative approaches to combating child labour: case studies from developing countries, *Innocenti Occasional Papers, Child Rights Series,* No. 8. Florence, Italy: United Nations Children's Fund, International Child Development Centre.

Boyden, Jo, Birgitta Ling, and William Myers (1998). *What Works for Working Children?* Stockholm and Florence, Italy: Rädda Barnen and UNICEF, International Child Development Centre.

Brooks-Gunn, Jeanne, Wen-Jui Han, and Jane Waldfogel (2002). Maternal employment and child cognitive outcomes in the first three years of life: the NICHD study of early childcare. *Child Development,* vol, 73, No. 4, pp. 1052-1072.

Buchmann, Claudia, and Emily Hannum (2001). Education and stratification in developing countries: a review of theories and research. *Annual Review of Sociology,* vol.27, pp. 77-102.

Business for Social Responsibility (2003). Monitoring of global supply chain practices, BSR issue briefs. Available from *http://www.bsr.org/.* April.

Campbell, Iain (2004). Casual work and casualisation: how does Australia compare? *Labour and Industry,* vol. 15, No. 2, pp. 85-111.

_____, and Peter Brosnan, (2005). Relative advantages: casual employment and casualisation in Australia and New Zealand. Paper presented at a conference on globalization and industrial relations reform in Australia and New Zealand, Sydney, February.

Chirwa, Ephraim, and others (2004). Study to inform the selection of an appropriate wage rate for public works programmes in Malawi. Report submitted to the National Safety Nets Unit, Government of Malawi.

Cigno, A., F. Rosati and L. Guarcello (2002). Does globalization increase child labor? *World Development*, vol. 30, No. 9, pp. 1579-1589.

Coady, David (2004). Designing and evaluating social safety nets: theory, evidence and policy conclusions. FCND Discussion Paper, No.172. Washington, D.C.: International Food Policy Research Institute, Food Consumption and Nutrition Division.

Coopersmith, Jared (2006). Inequality among professionals: the case of Brazilian schoolteachers. *Sociological Viewpoints, vol.22 (spring), pp.21-32.*

Cornia, Giovanni Andrea (1999). *Social Funds in Stabilization and Adjustment Programmes.* Working Paper, No. 48, Sales No. E.99.III.A.27. Helsinki: United Nations University/World Institute for Development Economics Research.

Curtain, Richard (2006). For poor countries' youth, dashed hopes signal danger ahead. *Current History*, vol. 105, No. 695 (December), pp. 435-440.

Daly, Mary, ed. (2001). *Care Work: The Quest for Security.* Geneva: International Labour Office.

Dehejia, Rajeev H., and Roberta Gatti (2002). Child labor: the role of income variability and access to credit across countries, NBER Working Paper, No. 9018. Cambridge Massachusetts: National Bureal of Economic Research.

Demeke, Mulat, Fantu Guta and Tadele Ferede (2003). Growth, employment, poverty and policies in Ethiopia: an empirical investigation. Issues in Employment and Poverty Discussion Paper, No. 12, Geneva: International Labour Office.

Department for International Development (2006). Social protection and economic growth in poor countries. Social Protection Briefing Note Series, No. 4. London, United Kingdom. Department for International Development.

Dev, M. (1995). India's Maharashtra Employment Guarantee Scheme: lessons from long experience, In *Employment and Poverty Reduction and* J. von Braun ed., *Food Security*, Washington, D.C.: International Food Policy Research Institute, pp. 108-143.

Devereux, S. (2005). Can minimum wages contribute to poverty reduction in poor countries? *Journal of International Development*, vol. 17, No. 7, pp. 899-912.

Dhanani, Shafiq, and Iyannatul Islam (2004). *Indonesian Wage Structure and Trends, 1976-2000.* ILO, Socio-Economic Security Programme policy paper. Geneva: International Labour Office.

Dickson, Tim (2002). The financial case for behaving responsibly. *Financial Times*, 19 August, p. 9.

Donelan, Karen, and others (1999). The cost of health system change: public discontent in five nations. *Health Affairs,* vol. 18, No. 3, pp. 205-216.

Dumont, Jean-Christophe and Thomas Liebig (2005). Labour market integration of immigrant women: overview and recent trends. Organization for Economic Cooperation and Development, Migrant Women and the Labour Market:

Diversity and Challenges: OECD and European Commission Seminar, Brussels, 26 and 27 September 2005. OECD room document, No. 3.

Easterly, William, Jozef Ritzan and Michael Woolcock (2006). Social cohesion, institutions and growth. Center for Global Development Working Paper, No. 94. Washington, D.C.: Center for global Development. August.

Eberstadt, N. (2005). Ageing in low-income countries: looking to 2025. In *World Economic Forum: The Global Competitiveness Report 2005-2006*. Basingstoke, United Kingdom: Palgrave Macmillan, Ltd, pp. 163-178.

European Commission (2001). The employment situation of people with disabilities in the European Union. Study prepared by EIM Business and Policy Research. Brussels: European Commission.

Evans, M., and others (2006). How progressive is social security in Vietnam? *Bath, United Kingdom:* University of Bath, Mimeo.

Fallon, Peter and Zafiris Tzannatos (1998). *Child Labor. Issues and Directions for the World Bank*, Washington, DC.: World Bank.

Feng, G. ed. (2001). *Twenty-first Century Chinese Urban Social Security System.* Zhengzhou, China: Henan Remin Chubanshe.

Financial Times (2006). Migrants mean money, Editorial comment, 31 July.

Forde, C., and G. Slater (2005). Agency working in Britain: character, consequences and regulation. *British Journal of Industrial Relations*, vol. 43, No. 2, pp. 249-271.

Frickey, Alan, Jake Murdoch and Jean-Luc Primon (2006). From higher education to employment: inequalities among ethnic backgrounds in France. *European Education*, vol. 37, No. 4, (winter).

Fryer, David, and Desire Vencatachellum (2005). Returns to education in South Africa: evidence from the Machibisa Township. *African Development Review,* vol. 17, No. 3 (December); pp. 513-535.

Fuentes, J. (1997). Sugerencias de políticas para la integración de los sectores informales, de micro y pequenos empresarios. Lima, Peru: International Labour Office. Documento de trabajo.

Fugazzo, Marco (2003). Racial discrimination: theories, facts and policy. *International Labour Review,* vol. 142, No. 4 (December), pp. 507-541.

Fuller, Sylvia, and Leah F. Vosko (2005). Temporary employment and social inequality in Canada. Paper presented at the workshop on economic security and casualisation, University of North British Columbia, 14-18 September.

Fyfe, Alec, and Michele Jankanish (1997). *Trade Unions and Child Labour: A Guide to Action*, ILO Child Labour Collection. Geneva: International Labour Office.

Gaiha, Raghav, and Katsushi Imai (2005). A review of the Employment Guarantee Scheme in India. Policy Case Study, Labour Markets and Employment, Inter-Regional Inequality Facility, Overseas Development Institute. 11 July. Available from *http://www.odi.org.uk/inter-regional_inequality/papers/Labour_marketw&employment(India).* pdf.

Ghosh, Bimal (2006). *Migrants' Remittances and Development: myths, rhetoric and realities.* Geneva: International Organisation for Migration. Available from *www.iom.int* (accessed 26 June 2007).

Global Commission on International Migration (2005). Migration in an interconnected world: new directions for action. Report of the Global Commission on International Migration. Geneva. October.

Goetz, Anne Marie, and Rina Sen Gupta (1996). Who takes the credit? gender, power and control over loan use in rural credit programmes in Bangladesh. *World Development*, vol. 24, No. 1, pp. 45-63.

Gordon, Ann, and Catherine Craig (2001). *Rural Non-Farm Activities and Poverty Alleviation in sub-Saharan Africa.* National Resource Institute Policy Series 14. Chatham, United Kingdom: Natural Resources Institute.

Görg, Holger, and Eric Strobl (2003). "Footloose" multinationals? *Manchester School*, vol. 71, No. 1, pp. 1-19.

Gottfried, H., M. Nishiwara and K. Aiba (2006). *Pathways to economic security*: gender and non-standard employment in contemporary Japan. Paper presented at the workshop on economic security and casualisation, University of North British Columbia, 14-18 September.

Gradstein, Mark,and Maurice Schiff (2006). The political economy of social exclusion with implications for immigration policy. *Journal of Population Economics*, vol. 19, No. 2, pp. 327-344.

Grimsrud, Bjørne. (2003). Millennium Development Goals and child labour, Understanding Children's Work: An Inter-Agency Research Cooperation Project of ILO, UNICEF, and World Bank Group. 23 October. Available from www.ucw-project.org/pdf/publications/mdg_and_cl.pdf (accessed 20 December, 2006).

Grootaert, C., and R. Kanbur (1995). Child labour: an economic perspective. *International Labour Review*, vol. 134, No. 2, pp. 187-203.

Groshen, Erica L., and Simon Potter (2003). Has structural change contributed to a jobless recovery? New York: Federal Reserve Bank of New York. *Current Issues in Economics and Finance*, vol. 9, No. 8, pp. 1-7.

Gurr, Ted (1993). *Minorities at Risk. A Global View of Ethnopolitical Conflicts.* Washington, D.C.: United States Institute of Peace Press.

_____(2000). *Peoples versus States: Minorities at Risk in the New Century.* Washington, D.C.: United State Institute for Peace Press.

Hall, G., and H.A. Patrinos (2006). *Indigenous Peoples, Poverty and Human Development in Latin America: 1994-2004,* New York: Palgrave Macmillan, Ltd.

Hamil-Luker, Jenifer (2005). Women's wages: cohort differences in returns to education and training over time. *Social Science Quarterly*, vol. 86, No. s1 (December), pp. 1261-1278.

Harford, Tim (2006). *The Undercover Economist: Exposing Why the Rich Are Rich, the Poor Are Poor--and Why You Can Never Buy a Decent Used Car!* Oxford, United Kingdom, and New York: Oxford University Press.

Harrison, A. (2002). Has globalization eroded labour's share? some cross country evidence. Cambridge, Massachusetts, and Berkeley. California: National Bureau of Economic Research, and University of California, Berkeley. Available from *http://wbln0018.worldbank.org/LAC/LACInfoClinet.nsf/ d29684951174975c8526735007fe12/7a6badb2c8df829785256c67005660cd/ $FILE/Harrison%20Has%20Eroded%20Labors%20Share.pdf*

_____, and G.H. Hanson (1999). Who gains from trade reform? Some remaining puzzles. *Journal of Development Economics*, vol. 59, No. 1, pp. 125-154.

Haspels, N., F. de los Angeles-Bautista, and V. Rialp (2000). Alternatives to child labour. In *Action against child labour*. Nelien Haspels and Michele Jankanish, eds. Geneva: International Labour Office.

Haspels, N., M. Romeijn and S. Schroth (2000). Promoting gender equality in action against child labour: a practical guide. Bangkok: International Labour Organization, regional office for Asia and the Pacific.

Hirschman, A.O (1970). *Exit, Voice and Loyalty*. Cambridge, Massachusetts: Harvard University Press.

Hirway, Indira, and Piet Terhal (1994). *Towards Employment Guarantee in India: Indian and International Experiences in Rural Public Works Programmes*. New Delhi: Sage Publications.

Hoekman, B., and L.A. Winters (2005). Trade and employment: stylised facts and research findings. World Bank Policy Research Working Paper, No. 3444. Washington, D.C.: World Bank.

Hopkins, Michael J.D. (1998). *The Planetary Bargain: Corporate Social Responsibility Comes of Age*. London: Macmillan.

_____(2006). *Corporate Social Responsibility and International Development*. London: Earthscan.

Ilahi, Nadeem (2001). Children's work and schooling: does gender matter? evidence from the Peru LSMS Panel data. Paper prepared for the Policy Research Report on Gender. Washington, D.C.: World Bank. December.

International Labour Organization (2002a). *Women and Men in the Informal Economy: A Statistical Picture*. Geneva: International Labour Office/Employment Sector.

_____ (2002b). Every child counts: new global estimates on child labour, Geneva: International Labour Office. April.

_____ (2003a) *Working out of Poverty: Report of the Director General*. International Labour Conference, 91st Session 2003. Geneva: International Labour Office.

_____ (2003b) *ILO Convention on indigenous and tribal peoples, 1989, No. 169*: A Manual. Geneva: International Labour Office.

_____ (2003c) Decent work in agriculture. Geneva: International Labour Office.

_____ (2003d). Information note on corporate social responsibility and international labour standards: third item on the agenda of the Working Party on the Social Dimension of Globalisation, Governing Body, Internaltional Labour

Office, 288th Session. GB.288/WP/SDG3. Geneva: November. Available from *http://www.ilo.org/public/english/standards/relm/gb/docs/gb288/pdf/sdg-3.pdf*.

_____ (2004a). *Economic Security for a Better World*. Geneva: International Labour Organization Socio-Economic Security Programme.

_____ (2004b). Trade, foreign investment and productive employment in developing countries. International Labour Office Governing Body Committee on Employment and Social Policy paper GB.291/ESP/2. Geneva: International Labour Office.

_____ (2004c). *Towards a Fair Deal for Migrant Workers in the Global Economy*. Report VI for the 92nd session of the International Labour Conference. Geneva: International Labour Office.

_____ (2005). *HIV/AIDS and Work in a Globalizing World*. The ILO Programme on HIV/AIDS and the World of Work. Geneva: International Labour Office.

_____ (2006a). *Changing Patterns in the World of Work*. Geneva: International Labour Office.

_____ (2006b). *The end of child labour: Within Reach*. Global report under the follow-up to the ILO Declaration on Fundamental Principles and Rights at Work. Report I (B) of the 95th session of the International Labour Conference. Geneva: International Labour Offiice.

_____ (2006c). *Global Employment Trends for Youth*. Geneva: International Labour Offiice.

_____ (2006d). ILO welcomes new UN Convention on rights of people with disabilities. Department of Communication press release, 14 December, International Labour Office. Available from: *http://www.ilo.org/public/english/bureau/inf/pr/2006/58.htm*.

_____ (2006e). *Guidelines for Combating Child Labour among Indigenous and Tribal Peoples*. Geneva: International Labour Office.

_____ (2007). *Equality at Work: Tackling the Challenges*. Report I (B) of the Director-General for the 96th session of the International Labour Conference. Geneva: International Labour Office.

Jankanish, M. (2000). Towards improved legislation. In *Action against child labour*. N. Haspels and M. Jankanish, eds. Geneva: International Labour Office.

Joint United Nations Programme on HIVAIDS (UNAIDS) (2004). *2004 Report on the Global AIDS Epidemic*. Geneva: UNAIDS, p. 15.

Jomo, K.S. (2006). Growth with equity in East Asia? DESA working papers series, No. ST/ESA/2006/DWP/33. September.

Justino, Patricia (2005). Beyond HEPR: a framework for an integrated national system of social security in Vietnam. Report for the United Nations Development Programme,. Policy Dialogue Paper 2005/1. Hanoi.

Kabeer, Naila (2001). Safety nets and opportunity ladders: addressing vulnerability and enhancing productivity in South Asia. *Development Policy Review*, vol.20, No.5, pp.589-614.

Kling, Jeffrey R. (2006). Fundamental restructuring of unemployment insurance: wage-loss insurance and temporary earnings replacement accounts. Discussion paper 2006-05. Washington, D.C.: The Hamilton Project, the Brookings Institution. September.

Kolev, Alexandre, and Catherine Saget (2005). Understanding youth labour market disadvantage: evidence from South-East Europe. *International Labour Review* vol. 144, No. 2, pp. 161-187.

KPMG (2002). KPMB International Survey of Corporate Sustainability Reporting 2002. Second printing, 24 June 2002. Amsterdam: University of Amsterdam, Amsterdam Graduate Business School. Available from *www.globalreporting. org*; or from *http://www.wimm.nl/publicaties/kpmg2002.pdf*

Kwa, Aileen (2001). Agriculture in developing countries: which way forward? South Centre, Trade-Related Agenda, Development and Equity Occasional Papers, No. 4, Geneva. June.

Lapper, Richard (2006). Inflow of dollars helps build good roads to empty future. *Financial Times*, 20 June.

_____, and Adam Thomson (2006). Peso power brings hope to poor, *Financial Times*, 29 June.

Lee, Eddy (2005). Trade liberalization and employment. DESA Working Paper Series, No. ST/ESA/2005/DWP/5. October.

Lee, Kang-kook, and Arjun Jayadev (2005). Capital account liberalization, growth and the labour share of income: reviewing and extending the cross-country evidence. In *Capital Flight and Capital Controls in Developing Countries*, Gerald Epstein, ed., Cheltenham, United Kingdom: Edward Elgar, pp. 15-57.

Lee, Sangheon, Deidre McCann and Jon C. Messenger (2007). *Working Time Around the World: Trends in Working Hours, Laws, and Policies in a Global Comparative Perspective*. London and Geneva: Routledge and International Labour Office.

Lee, William Keng Mun (2004). The economic marginality of ethnic minorities: an analysis of ethnic income inequality in Singapore. *Asian Ethnicity*, vol. 5, No. 1 (February).

Lemieux, Thomas (2006). Post-secondary education and increasing wage inequality. *American Economic Review*. vol. 96, No. 2 (May).

Lethbridge, Jane (2006). Implications of healthcare liberalization for workers' security, In *Winners or Losers? Liberalising Public Services*, Evelyne Rosskam, ed. Geneva: International Labour Office.

Levy Economics Institute, Bard College, and United Nations Development Programme, (2006). Proceedings of the Global Conference on Unpaid Work and the Economy: Gender, Poverty and the Millennium Development Goals, 1-3 October, 2005. Annandale-on-Hudson, New York.

Lichbach, M. I. (1989). An evaluation of "Does economic inequality breed political conflict?" *World Politics*, vol. 41; No. 4 (July), pp. 431-470.

Lothike, Eris (2005). Experiences from Turkana 2001 and 2003. Paper presented at the meeting organized by the Overseas Development Institute and the Great Lakes and East Africa Inter-Agency Emergency and Preparedness Working Group, Nairobi, 11 May.

Marx, Ive (2005). Job subsidies and cuts in employers' social security contributions: the verdict of empirical evaluation studies. Paper presented at the conference on Changing Social Policies for Low-Income Families and Less-Skilled Workers in the E.U. and the U.S., University of Michigan, 7 and 8 April 2005. Ann Arbor, Michigan.

Matin, Imran, David Hulme and Stuart Rutherford (1999). *Financial services for the poor and poorest: Deepening understanding to improve provision.* Finance and Development Research Programme, Working Paper Series, No. 9. Manchester, United Kingdom: Institute for Development Policy and Management, University of Manchester. Available from *http://www.cmfnet. org.za/Documents/Financial%20Services%20For@20The%20Poor%20and% 20Poorest.doc.*

McCord, Anna (2003). *An Overview of the Performance and Potential of Public Works Programmes in South Africa.* University of Cape Town, Centre for Social Science Research Working Paper, No. 0349. Cape Town: University of Cape Town.

_____(2004). *Policy Expectations and Programme Reality: The Poverty Reduction and Labour Market Impact of Two Public Works Programmes in South Africa.* ESAU Working Paper No. 8. London: Overseas Development Institute, Economic and Statistics Analysis Unit.

_____(2005a). A critical evaluation of training within the South African National Public Works Programme, *Journal of Vocational Education and Training*, vol. 57, No. 4.

_____(2005b). *Public Works in the Context of HIV/AIDS: Innovations in Public Works for Reaching the Most Vulnerable Children and Households in East and Southern Africa.* Cape Town: South African Labour and Development Research Unit, Public Works Research Project, School of Economics, University of Cape Town.

McKenzie, D.J (2006). Beyond remittances: the effects of migration on Mexican households. In *International Migration, Remittances and the Brain Drain*, C. Ozden and M. Schiff, eds. Washington D.C.: World Bank and Palgrave MacMillan, pp. 123-147.

Metts, Robert L. (2003). Thinking outside of the net: the effective use of social safety nets in national disability policy. World Bank event on Protecting the Vulnerable: The Design and Implementation of Effective Safety Nets, 1-12 December 2002, Washington, D.C.

Milanovic, B., and L. Squire (2005). Does trade liberalization increase wage inequality? Some empirical evidence. NBER Working Paper; No. 11046. Cambridge, Massachusetts: National Bureau of Economic Research.

Moore, Karen (2000). Supporting children in their working lives: obstacles and opportunities within the international policy environment. *Journal of International Development*, vol. 12, No. 4, pp. 531-548.

Moran, T., E. Graham, and Blomstrom, M. (eds.)(2005). *Does Foreign Direct Investment Promote Development?* Washington, D.C.: Institute for International Economics.

Mroz, Thomas A., and Timothy H. Savage (2001). The long term effects of youth unemployment. Washington, D.C.: Employment Policies Institute.

Muller, Edward N. (1995). Income inequality and democratization: reply to Bollen and Jackman. *American Sociological Review*, vol. 60, No. 6 (December).

Nkurunziza, Janvier D. (2006). Generating rural employment in Africa to fight poverty. Paper presented at the ECOSOC high-level segment, 8-9 May, New York.

O'Reilly, Arthur (2004). *Equity Issues: The Right to Decent Work of Persons with Disabilities*. Skills Working Paper, No. 14. Geneva: International Labour Office.

Organization for Economic Cooperation and Development (2002). *OECD Employment Outlook 2002: Surveying the Jobs Horizon*. Paris: Organization for Economic Cooperation and Development Publications Service.

Organization for Economic Cooperation and Development (2003). *Transforming Disability into Ability: Policies to Promote Work and Income Security for Disabled People*. Paris: Organization for Economic Cooperation and Development, OECD Publications Service.

_____ (2006). The share of employment potentially affected by offshoring: an empirical investigation. Working Party on the Information Economy, Directoriate for Science, Technology and Industry, Committee for Information, Computer and Communications Policy. DSTI/ICCP/IE(2005)8/FINAL. Paris: OECD. February. Available from: *http://www.oecd.org/dataoecd/37/26/36187829.pdf*. (accessed 25 May 2007).

Orszag, J. Michael, and Dennis J. Snower (2002). From unemployment benefits to unemployment accounts. Institute for the Study of Labour Discussion Paper, No. 532. Bonn.

Osmani, S. (1997). Empowerment and drudgery: trade-offs for poor rural women. Paper presented at the Workshop on Gender Differentials in Work Intensity, Sustainability and Development, University of East Anglia, Norwich, United Kingdom.

Osmani, S.R. (2003). Exploring the employment nexus: topics in employment and poverty. Report prepared for the Task Force on the Joint ILO-UNDP Programme on Employment and Poverty. June, p. 27.

Özden, Çaglar and Maurice Schiff, eds. (2005). *International Migration, Remittances and the Brain Drain*. Washington, D.C.: Palgrave Macmillan and World Bank.

Pan American Health Organization (2006). Disabilities: what everyone should know. The Newsletter of the Pan American Health Organization Promoting Health in the Americas, August 2006. Available from *http://www.paho.org/English/DD/PIN/ptoday17_aug06.htm* (accessed 24 June 2007).

Pavcnik, N., and others (2002). Trade liberalization and labour market adjustment in Brazil. World Bank Policy Research Working Paper, No. 2982. Washington, D.C.: World Bank.

Paxson, Christina, and Norbert R. Schady (2002). The allocation and impact of social funds: spending on school infrastructure in Peru. *World Bank Economic Review*, vol. 16, No. 2, pp. 297-319.

Quisumbing, Agnes R. (2003). Food aid and child nutrition in rural Ethiopia. *World Development*, vol. 31, No. 7, pp. 1309-1324.

Rahman, Aminur (1999). Microcredit initiatives for equitable and sustainable development: who pays? *World Development*, vol. 27, No. 1, pp. 67-82.

Ram, Rati (2006). Further examination of the cross-country association between income inequality and population health. *Social Science and Medicine* (Oxford: United Kingdom): vol. 62, No. 3 (February).

Ravallion, Martin (1999). Appraising workfare. *World Bank Research Observer*, vol. 14, No. 1 (February).

_____, and Q. Wodon (2000). Does child labour displace schooling? evidence on behavioural responses to an enrollment Subsidy. *The Economic Journal*, vol. 110, No. 462 (March), pp. 158-175.

Reardon, Thomas, and others (1998). Rural non-farm income in developing countries. In *The State of Food and Agriculture 1998*. Rome: Food and Agriculture Organization of the UN, part III.

Right to Food Campaign (2005). Overview of the National Rural Employment Guarantee Act 2005. Available from *http://www.righttofoodindia.org/* (accessed 29 June 2007).

Rocha, Sonia (2000). Applying minimum income programmes in Brazil: two case studies: Belem and Belo Horizonte. IPEA, Discussion Paper, No. 746. Rio de Janeiro: Institute for Applied Economic Research.

Rosskam, Ellen ed. (2006). *Winners or Losers? Liberalising Public Services.* Geneva: International Labour Office.

Rudra, Nita (2004). Openness, welfare spending, and inequality in the developing world. *International Studies Quarterly*, vol. 48, No. 3, pp. 683-709.

Sabates-Wheeler, Rachel, and Naila Kabeer (2003). *Gender equality and the extension of social protection.* International Labour Organization, Extension of Social Security Paper, No.16, Geneva: International Labour Office.

Samson, Michael, Ingrid van Niekerk and Kenneth MacQuene (2006). *Designing and Implementing Social Transfer Programmes.* Cape Town: Economic Policy Research Institute.

Schock, Kurt (1996). A conjunctural model of political conflict: the impact of political opportunities on the relationship between economic inequality and violent political conflict. *The Journal of Conflict Resolution*, vol. 40, No. 1 (March).

Sconnes, Ian, and William Wolmer, eds. (2003). *Livelihoods in Crisis? New Perspectives on Governance and Rural Development in Southern Africa. IDS Bulletin;* vol. 34; No. 3 (July). Brighton, United Kingdom: Institute of Development Studies, University of Sussex. Further information available from *http://www.ids. ac.uk/ids/bookshop/bulletin/bullere.htm*

Sheve, Kenneth F. and Matthew J. Slaughter (2002). Economic insecurity and the globalization of production. NBER Working Paper, No. 9339. Cambridge, Massachusetts: National Bureau of Economic Research.

Slaughter, Matthew J. (2001). International trade and labour-demand elasticities, *Journal of International Economics*, vol. 54, No. 1, pp. 27-56.

Social Investment Forum (n.d.). Report on socially responsible investing trends in the United States. Available from *www.socialinvest.org*

Standing, Guy (2002). *Beyond the New Paternalism: Basic Security as Equality*. London: Verso.

_____ (2006). Labour flexibility in Chinese enterprises. Melbourne, Australia: University of Monash. Mimeo.

_____, John Sender and John Weeks (1996*). Restructuring the Labour Market: The South African Challenge*. An ILO Country Review. Geneva: International Labour Organization.

Stewart, Francis, and Willem van der Geest (1994). Adjustment and social funds: political panacea or effective poverty reduction? International Development Centre, Oxford, United Kingdom.

Subbarao, Kalanidhi (2003). Systemic shocks and social protection: role and effectiveness of public works programs. Social Protection Discussion Paper, No. 0302. Washington, D.C.: World Bank.

_____, and others (1997). *Safety Net Programs and Poverty Reduction: Lessons from Cross-Country Experience*. Washington, DC: World Bank.

Swaminathan, Madhura (1998). Economic growth and the persistence of child labor: evidence from an Indian city. *World Development*, vol. 26, No. 8, pp. 1513-1528.

Sylva, Kathy (2004). Interventions that work. In *Moral Development in the Toddler Year*, N. Fox, ed. New York: Johnson and Johnson.

Sylwester, Kevin (2000). Can education expenditures reduce income inequality. *Economics of Education Review*, vol. 21, No. 1, pp. 43-52.

Tabusa, S. (2000). Trade unions against child labour. In: *Action Against Child Labour*, N. Haspels and M. Jankanish, eds. Geneva: International Labour Office.

Taran, Patrick, and Edouardo Geronimi (2003). *Globalisation, Labour and Migration: Protection is Paramount*. Geneva: International Labour Office.

Thomas, V., ed. (2001). *Traditional Occupations of Indigenous and Tribal Peoples: Emerging Trends*. Project to Promote ILO Policy on Indigenous and Tribal Peoples. Geneva: International Labour Office.

Tokman, Victor E. (2006). Integrating the informal sector in the modernization process. Paper presented at the DESA Forum on Productive Employment and Decent Work, 8 and 9 May, 2006, United Nations Headquarters, New York.

United Nations (2001). Report of the World Conference against Racism, Racial Discrimination, Xenophobia and Related Intolerance. Durban, South Africa, 31 August - 8 September 2001. A.CONF.189/12 and Corr.1, Chap. I.

_____ (2002a). *World Population Ageing 1950-2050*. Sales No. E.02.XIII.3, United Nations Publications.

_____ (2002b). World Youth Report 2003: *The Global Situation of Young People*, report of the Secretary-General. E/CN.5/2003/4. 12 December.

_____ (2004a). *World Youth Report 2003*. Sales No. #.03.IV.7.

_____ (2004b). Implementation of the United Nations Millennium Declaration: report of the Secretary-General. A/59/282 and Corr.1. 27 August.

_____ (2004c). World Youth Report 2005. report of the Secretary-General. A/60/61 – E/2005/7.

_____ (2004d). Review of the implementation of the Beijing Platform of Action and the outcome documents of the special session of the General Assembly, entitled "Women 2000: gender equality development and peace for the twenty-first century: report of the Secretary General. E/CN.6/2005/2 And Corr.1.

_____ (2005) *The Inequality Predicament: Report on the World Social Situation, 2005*. Sales No. E.05.IV.5.

_____ (2006a). World population monitoring, focusing on international migration and development: report of the Secretary-General E/CN.9/2006/3.

_____ (2006b). International migration and development: report of the Secretary-General to the 60th session of the UN General Assembly. A/60/871. New York, May.

_____ (2006c). Follow-up to the World Programme of Action for Youth: report of the Secretary-General. A/60/61 – E/2005/7.

_____ (2006d). General Major developments in the area of ageing since the Second World Assembly on Ageing: report of the Secretary. E/CN.5/2007/7 and Corr.1.

_____ (2006e). Convention on the Rights of Persons with Disabilities: some fact about persons with disabilities and the optional protocol thereto. Available from *http://www.un.org/disabilities/convention/facts.shtml*

_____ (2006f). UN Declaration on the Rights of Indigenous Peoples. General Assembly resolution 61/178 of 20 December 2006, annex.

_____ (2006g). Convention on the Rights of Persons with Disabilities. General Assembly resolution 61/106 of 13 December 2006, annex I and II.

_____ (2006h). *Building Inclusive Financial Sectors for Development*. Sales No. E.06. II.A.3.

_____ (2007). *World Economic and Social Survey 2007*: *Development in an Ageing World*. UN, ESCAP and UN, ECLAC. Sales No. E.07.II.C.1.

_____ Economic and Social Commission for Asia and the Pacific (2005). Economic and Social Survery for Asia and the Pacific, *2005: Dealing with Shocks*. ST/ESCAP/2349. Sales No. E.05.II.F.10, p. 243. Bangkok: Economic and Social Commission for Asia and the Pacific.

_____(2006). Disability at a Glance: A Profile of 28 Countries and Areas in Asia and the Pacific. ST/ESCAP/2421. Sales No. E.06.ii.F.24. Bangkok: Economic and Social Commission for Asia and the Pacific.

_____United Nations, Economic Commission for Latin America and the Caribbean (2004). Social Panorama of Latin America, 2004. Sales No. E.04.II.G.148, p.123.

United Nations Children's Fund (2004). *The State of the World's Children.* New York: UNICEF. 2005.

_____ (2005). *The State of the World's Children,* 2006. New York: UNICEF.

United Nations Conference on Trade and Development (2006). *The Least Developed Countries Report 2006: Developing Productive Capacities.* Sales No.: E.06.II.D.9.

United Nations Development Programme (2005a). *Arab Human Development Report 2004.* April. Available from: *http://www.rbas.undp.org/ahdr2004.shtml.*

_____ (2005b). *Human Development Report 2005.* Sales No. E.05.III.B.1.

United Nations Educational, Scientific and Cultural Organization (2004). Who are excluded and why? Education for All Week, 19-25 April 2004. Available from: *http://portal.unesco.org/education/en/ev.php-URL_ID=28705&URL_DO=DO_TOPIC&URL_SECTION=201.html.*

_____ (2006). Global Education Digest 2006: Comparing Education Statistics Across the World. Montreal, Quebec, Canada: UNESCO Institute for Statistics.

United Nations Office of the High Representative for the Least Developed Countries, Landlocked Developing Countries and Small Island Developing States, and Office of the Special Adviser on Africa (2006). *Migrant workers' remittances in Africa and LDCs:* A new development paradigm. New York. Available from *http://www.un.org/special-rep/ohrlls/Press_release/issue%20paper-%remittances%20_OHRLLS-OSAA.pdf.*

United Nations Population Fund (2006). *State of World Population 2006: A Passage to Hope: Women and International Migration.* Sales No. E.06.III.H.1. p. 1.

Unni, Jeemol, and Uma Rani (2002). *Insecurities of informal workers in Gujarat, India.* Paper No.30. Geneva: International Labour Office.

van Beers, Cees and André de Moor (2001). *Public Subsidies and Policy Failures: How Subsidies Distort the Natural Environment, Equity and Trade and How to Reform Them.* Northampton, United Kingdom: Edward Elgar.

van der Hoeven, Rolph, and Malta Lubker (2006). External openness and employment: the need for coherent international and national policies. Paper prepared for the Development Forum on Productive Employment and Decent Work. United Nations, New York, May 2006.

van der Lippe, Tanja, and L. van Dijk (2002). Comparative research on women's employment. *Annual Review of Sociology,* vol. 28, pp. 221-241.

Wachtel, H. (2003). Tax distortion in the global economy, In *Global Tensions: Challenges and Opportunities in the World Economy,* L. Beneria and S. Bisneth eds. New York and London: Routledge, pp. 27-43.

Waldfogel, Jane, Wen-Jui Han and Jeanne Brooks-Gunn (2002). The effects of early maternal employment on child cognitive development. *Demography*, vol. 39, No. 2, (May) pp. 369-92.

Weathers, C. (2001). Changing white-collar workplaces and female temporary workers in Japan. *Social Science Japan Journal*, vol. 4, No. 2, pp. 201-218.

Wells, Ryan (2006). Education's effect on income inequality: and economic globalization perspective. *Globalisation, Societies and Education*, vol. 4, No. 3 (November).

Williamson, John (2002). Proposals for Curbing the Boom-Bust Cycle in the Supply of Capital to Emerging Markets. United Nations University/World Institute for Development Economics Research Discussion Paper, No. 2002/3. Helsinki: UNU/WIDER. January.

Winters, L. Alan (2004). Trade liberalization and economic performance: an overview. *Economic Journal*, vol. 114, No. 493, pp. F4-F21.

Wolf, Martin (2006). How to harvest the disputed fruits of unskilled immigration, *Financial Times*, 5 April.

Woodhead, Martin (1998). *Children's Perspectives on their Working Lives: A Participatory Study in Bangladesh, Ethiopia, the Philippines, Guatemala, El Salvador and Nicaragua.*, Stockholm: Rädda Barnen.

World Bank (2005a). *Economic Growth in the 1990s: Learning from a Decade of Economic Reform*. Washington, D.C.

_____ (2005b). *Global Economic Prospects 2006: Economic Implications of Remittances and Migration*. Washington, D.C.: World Bank.

_____ (2006). *World Development Report 2007: Development and the Next Generation*. Washington, D.C. : World Bank.

World Food Programme (2006). *World Hunger Series 2006: Hunger and Learning*. Rome: World Food Programme and Palo alto, California, Stanford: Stanford University Press.

World Health Organization (2002) Active ageing: a policy framework.WHO/NMH/ NPH/02.8. Geneva: World Health Organization. Contribution of WHO to the Second World Assembly on Ageing, Madrid, April 2002.

_____ (2003). Access to rehabilitation for the 600 million people living with disabilities. WHO Media Centre. Available from: *http://www.who.int/ mediacentre/news/notes/2003/np24/en/* (accessed 13 June 2007).

International Labour Office and United Nations Educational, Scientific and Cultural Organization (2004). CBR: *A Strategy for Rehabilitation. Equalization of Opportunities, Poverty Reduction and Social Inclusion of People with Disabilities: Joint Position paper, 2004*. Geneva: World Health Organization.

World Trade Organization (2006). *World Trade Report 2006: Exploring the Links Between Subsidies, Trade and the WTO*. Geneva: World Trade Organization.

Zheng, Cheng Gon (2002). Zhongguo Shehui Baozhang Zhidu Bianqian Yu Pinggu (The evolution of China's social protection system and an appraisal). Beijing: Zhongguo Remin Daxue Chubanshe. People's University Press).